PENGUIN BOOKS

THE COMPLETE NONSENSE AND OTHER VERSE

Vivien Noakes is the author of the acclaimed biography *Edward Lear: The Life of a Wanderer* and *The Painter Edward Lear*. She edited *Edward Lear: Selected Letters* and was the Guest Curator of the major exhibition *Edward Lear 1812–1888* at the Royal Academy of Arts, London, and the National Academy of Design, New York.

EDWARD LEAR

The Complete Nonsense and Other Verse

Compiled and edited by
VIVIEN NOAKES

PENGUIN BOOKS

PENGUIN BOOKS

Published by the Penguin Group
Penguin Books Ltd, 80 Strand, London WC2R 0RL, England
Penguin Putnam Inc., 375 Hudson Street, New York, New York 10014, USA
Penguin Books Australia Ltd, 250 Camberwell Road, Camberwell, Victoria 3124, Australia
Penguin Books Canada Ltd, 10 Alcorn Avenue, Toronto, Ontario, Canada M4V 3B2
Penguin Books India (P) Ltd, 11 Community Centre, Panchsheel Park, New Delhi – 110 017, India
Penguin Books (NZ) Ltd, Cnr Rosedale and Airborne Roads, Albany, Auckland, New Zealand
Penguin Books (South Africa) (Pty) Ltd, 24 Sturdee Avenue, Rosebank 2196, South Africa

Penguin Books Ltd, Registered Offices: 80 Strand, London WC2R 0RL, England

www.penguin.com

This edition first published as *The Complete Verse and Other Nonsense*
by Allen Lane The Penguin Press 2001
Published under the present title, with a new introduction and omitting
other editorial matter, in Penguin Books 2002

3

Introduction copyright © Vivien Noakes, 2002
All rights reserved

The moral right of the editor has been asserted

Printed in England by Clays Ltd, St Ives plc

PRIVATE and KOMΦIDEMTIAL

Contents

Acknowledgements

I owe a great debt to earlier editors of Lear's nonsense, who not only made his work available to readers in their own time, but have, in some cases, preserved in their editions nonsense that has subsequently disappeared. Of special importance is Lady Strachey, the niece of Frances, Lady Waldegrave who was married to one of Lear's closest friends, Chichester Fortescue. At a time when Lear's reputation was at its lowest, she edited two volumes of correspondence between Lear and her aunt and Fortescue, as well as *Queery Leary Nonsense* (1911) and *The Complete Nonsense Book* (1912). Where some other families disposed of Lear material, she preserved theirs so that it would be available to later scholars. Holbrook Jackson's *The Complete Nonsense of Edward Lear* (1947) has delighted generations of children. My most vivid memory of this book is seeing it tucked under the arm of our Latin mistress as she came in for the last Latin lesson of each term. My joy in what she read was as great as my dislike of the subject she normally taught, and, although I had known his nonsense from earliest childhood, this was my real introduction to the delights of Edward Lear.

Work on this edition has been under way, as a background to other research into Lear's life and work, since 1963. Those years have seen the death of a number of people without whom it could not have been achieved. Foremost among these is Philip Hofer, whose collection of Lear manuscripts – together with those of William B. Osgood Field – was deposited at the Houghton Rare Book and Manuscript Library, Harvard University, in 1942, making possible much of the Lear scholarship that has followed; my debt to him, as a scholar and a friend, is incalculable. I would also like to record my deep gratitude to George Buday, Herbert Cahoon, Arnold Clark, Donald Gallup, William

Hornby, Sheila Kerr, Herman Liebert, Mr and Mrs Robert Gillies Michell, Colonel William Prescott, Edward Selwyn and Susan, Lady Tweedsmuir. I am sad that they cannot see the ways in which their generous help contributed to the finished edition.

I would like to extend my warm thanks to W. H. Bond and Eleanor Garvey who, as successive Curators of Printing and Graphic Arts at the Houghton Library, offered me every facility for research in their incomparable collection of manuscripts. I have shared much hospitality and conversation with Justin Schiller in New York and London, and his willingness to make material available to me meant that I knew of manuscripts I might otherwise have missed. It is with gratitude that I dedicate this book to him. Frederick Koch graciously allowed me free access to his collection of Leariana, much of which is now on deposit in the Beinecke Library. Sir Thomas Barlow, Bt, the Hon. Mrs A. Buchan, Dr David Michell and James Farquharson were most generous in allowing me to use material which has come down through their families. To Charles Lewsen I am grateful for the hours and the ideas we shared. For help in many ways I would like to thank George Ainscow, Sir David Attenborough, Malcolm Brown, Maldwin Drummond, Stephen Guy, Maureen Lambourne, Iona Opie, Gordon Sauer and Derek Wise.

The staff of a number of libraries and museums have been both patient and helpful. For this, and for permission to reproduce material in their collections, I would like to thank the Beinecke Rare Book and Manuscript Library at Yale University, the Berg Collection in the New York Public Library, Brigham Young University, the British Library, the Butler Library at Columbia University, Christie's International, the Syndics of the Fitzwilliam Museum, Cambridge, Mrs Arthur A. Houghton, Jr, the Houghton Rare Book and Manuscript Library at Harvard University, the Henry Huntington Library and Art Gallery, the National Library of Scotland, Penguin Books (the archives of Frederick Warne), the William R. Perkins Library at Duke University, the Pierpont Morgan Library, the Harry Ransom Humanities Research Center at the University of Texas at Austin, the Representative Church Body Library in Dublin, the University of Rochester Library, the Somerset Record Office, the Principal and Fellows of Somerville College, Oxford, the Robert Manning Strozier Library at Florida State University, Robert H. Taylor Collection, Department of Rare Books and Special Collections, Princeton University Library, the Tennyson Research

Centre at Lincoln, the Trustees of the Victoria and Albert Museum, and the Library of Westminster School. For permission to quote copyright material I would like to thank: the Trustees of Mrs C. H. A. Anstruther-Duncan for 'There was an old person whose legs', 'There was an old man whose delight', 'There was an old man who said,"See!"', 'There was an old man of Lodore', 'There was an old person so silly', 'There was an old man whose repose', 'There was an old man whose despair', 'There was an old person of Sidon', 'There was an old person whose mirth', 'There was an old lady of Leeds', 'There was an old man in a boat', 'There was an old man whose desire', 'There was an old person of Calais', 'There was an old man with a light', 'There was an old man who said "O! –' and 'There was an old man who made bold'; and Letters to Anna Duncan and Lady Duncan in *Bosh and Nonsense*; Faber and Faber Ltd for W. H. Auden's poem 'Edward Lear'; Fondation Martin Bodmer for 'Remminissenciz of Orgust 14 Aitnundrednaity' in *English and American Autographs in the Bodmeriana*; the Trustees of Lady Charnwood for 'Eggstrax from The Maloja Gazette' in *Call Back Yesterday*; James and Rosemary Farquharson for 'Eggstracts from the Roehampton Chronicle' in *Edward Lear: A New Nonsense Alphabet*; the late Denise Harvey for [Lear's adventures in Crete], plate 3, in *Edward Lear: The Cretan Journal*; H. P. Kraus, New York, for 'Oh! Pan!', second illustration to 'There was an Old Man of Nepaul', 'There was an old man who forgot', 'There was an old man of Orleans', 'There was an old man of the Dee' and 'There was an old person of Leith' in *Lear in the Original*; John Murray (Publishers) Ltd for drafts for a poem describing the later history of the Owl and the Pussy-cat in Angus Davidson, *Edward Lear: Landscape Painter and Nonsense Poet*, for 'Ribands and pigs', 'The Adventures of Mr Lear & the Polly [& the] Pusseybite on their way to the Ritertitle Mountains', 'Cold are the crabs that crawl on yonder hill' and [Nonsense Trees] in *Teapots and Quails*, and for [Lear's adventures on horseback], nos. 3, 4, 5, 10, 12, 14, 21, 25, 33, and 'The Hens of Oripò' in Susan Hyman *Edward Lear in the Levant*; *Poetry Review* for 'When the light dies away on a calm summer's eve' and 'From the pale and the deep'; the Royal Academy of Arts for 'I slept, and back to my early days', 'Portraites of the inditchenous beestes of New Olland', [Lear's adventures on horseback], nos. 2, 8, 26, 27, 'Object discovered in Beta' and 'O Digby my dear' in *Edward Lear 1812–1888: The Catalogue of the Royal Acade-*

my of Arts Exhibition; the Trustees of Hugh Sharp for 'The Pobble and Princess Bink'; and *Sussex County Magazine* for 'Peppering Roads'; the Victoria and Albert Museum for six coloured birds. I have established copyright for previously unpublished material in *Selected Letters*, and for the illustrations, 'Scene in the Campagna of Rome', 'Ye poppular author & traveller in Albania & Calabrià, keepinge his feete warme', 'There was an old man with a Book', 'O dear! how disgusting is life!', Letter to Mrs Stuart Wortley [The Moon Journey] and illustration from a letter to Hallam Tennyson of 16 June 1884 in *Edward Lear: The Life of a Wanderer*; and 'Miss Fraser's Album' in *The Painter Edward Lear*.

I would like to thank Professor Christopher Ricks, whose enthusiasm for Lear led to the proposal for this edition. Copy-editing is always an exacting discipline, but with Lear the problems are exaggerated and I am grateful to Lindeth Vasey for her punctilious attention to detail. My thanks go also to my editor, Margaret Bartley, and to the designer, Peter Stratton.

Finally, I am grateful to the Society of Authors whose grant enabled me to open Windows on the world.

I would like to dedicate this edition to Justin Schiller

Introduction

Edward Lear was born on 12 May 1812. He was the twentieth of twenty-one children. His father, Jeremiah Lear, was a successful London sugar-refiner and Master of the Fruiterers' Company, one of the City Livery Companies. But when Edward was about four, Jeremiah suffered a sudden financial collapse; it seems possible that he served a short prison sentence for debt.

Rejected by his mother, Edward was brought up by his oldest sister Ann. She was a jolly, affectionate woman whose positive approach to life helped to guide her brother through a troubled childhood. He suffered from short-sight, bronchitis and epilepsy, and from bouts of severe depression, but from his early years he responded to these problems by seeking out the humour in any situation. 'Nonsense is the breath of my nostrils' he once wrote and it became for him a philosophy of life. As a teenager he described himself as '3 parts crazy and wholly affectionate', for his was a gentle laughter, drawing on the folly of human actions and the absurdity of many of the conventions which ruled the society in which he lived. Throughout his life he sought to share this understanding of folly with others, especially children. He loved the company of young people and they responded happily to the tall, bespectacled, merry yet strangely sad man.

When he was fifteen and a half, Lear had to begin earning his own living and he did so by drawing and painting. Within a few years he had become one of the most celebrated ornithological draughtsman of his age, indeed some believe him to have been the finest that England has ever produced. At the age of nineteen he published *Illustrations of the Family of Psittacidae, or Parrots*, a book of fine, hand-coloured lithographs, and he went on to do many of the drawings for John Gould's early works. In about 1831 he met Lord Stanley, heir to the

Earl of Derby, who invited him to his home at Knowsley, near Liverpool, to make a record of the unusual and often exotic birds and animals in his celebrated private menagerie. Lear worked at Knowsley, on and off, for about six years, building up a wide circle of acquaintance and future patronage.

By the mid 1830s the damp English climate was affecting his health, and his already bad eyesight was deteriorating. He decided to give up the close, minutely detailed natural history work and to turn instead to landscape painting. Lord Derby encouraged him in his wish to go to Italy, and in 1837 Lear left England to become part of the international community of artists in Rome. It was the start of a lifetime of travel, around the Mediterranean and the Middle East and later in India.

He returned to England frequently, sometimes staying for just a few months, sometimes for a year or more, but after 1837 he lived most of his life abroad. During the 1840s he published three books describing and illustrating his travels around Rome and in 1846, as a result of seeing his book *Illustrated Excursions in Italy*, Queen Victoria invited him to give her a course of twelve drawing lessons. In the same year he published the first edition of *A Book of Nonsense*, a collection of limericks he had composed and illustrated to entertain the nurseryful of children at Knowsley.

His reputation as an artist grew slowly but he had never had any formal training, and when, in 1850, he received a legacy of £500 he decided to enrol as a student at the Royal Academy Schools. But the venture was not a success, and within months he was once more earning his living. As the decade went on his reputation grew and he began to demand considerable prices for his paintings. In 1861, a large, important painting of the Cedars of Lebanon on which he had been working, unpaid, for many months was exhibited in London. Lear had hoped that this work would confirm his reputation, but instead it was dismissed by a critic writing in *The Times* and remained unsold. This was the turning point of his career; from then on he would come to rely increasingly on the patronage of friends. Yet, during these later years of apparent failure he was to produce some of his finest work.

He lived for some years in Corfu, returning to England each summer to exhibit his paintings. In the late 1860s he began to winter in the south of France and in 1870 built himself a house on the Italian

Riviera where he lived, alone apart from his servant Giorgio and his tailless cat Foss, for the rest of his life. It was a solitary existence, but out of this loneliness grew some of his most enduring nonsense; indeed it is possible that had he been a successful and sought-after painter, he might never have written his greatest nonsense songs.

Lear was not a professional writer; his nonsense was an always absurd and sometimes joyous means of self-expression. He had many friends but he told no one of his epilepsy, a lifelong habit of secrecy which set him apart and drew from him an understanding of the value of tolerance towards those who are different. 'The Owl and the Pussy-cat', his most famous nonsense song, was written in 1867 for a small child who was ill in bed. Like the Jumblies, these two creatures had the courage to face a hazardous journey into an unknown which brought with it the excitement of new worlds. Over the next nine years Lear created adventures for many more strange, enduring creatures - the Yonghy-Bonghy-Bò, the Quangle Wangle, the Jumblies, the Pobble who has no toes and the Dong with a luminous nose.

He died alone in San Remo on 29 January 1888. It would be near-ly a century before his reputation as a painter was established beyond doubt. His standing as 'The Father of Nonsense', a title which delight-ed him, has always been beyond question.

The Complete Nonsense
and Other Verse

Eclogue

Vide Collins 'Hassan – or the Camel Driver'

In dreary silence down the bustling road
The Lears – with all their goods and chattels rode;
Ten carts of moveables went on before,
And in the rear came half-a-dozen more;
A Hackney-coach the Lears themselves enshrouds
To guard them from the gaze of vulgar crowds.
The vehicle has reached the turnpike gate, –
Where wond'ring toll-men, – throngs of people wait; –
The loaded carts their dusty way pursue, –
Shrill squeak the wheels, – dark London was in view.   10
With grief heart-rending then, those mournful folk
Thrice sighed – thrice wiped their eyes – as thus they
        spoke:
'Sad was the hour – and luckless was the day
When first from Bowman's Lodge we bent our way! –

'How little half the woes can we foresee,
Of that thrice odious New Street where we flee! –
Bethink thee Mother! – can we ever find
Half room enough for all these goods behind? –
Soon must those carts their precious loads resign, –
Then, what but noise and trouble shall be thine! –   20
Ye banished furnitures, that once did bear
In our last Halls a more than equal share,
Here, where no dark rooms shew their craving door,
Or mildewed lumberrooms make place for more,
In vain ye hope the comfort – space – to know,
Which dark rooms large or lumberrooms bestow, –
Here closets only – dwarfish rooms are found,
And scanty inconvenience rules around.
Sad was the hour and luckless was the day
When first from Bowman's Lodge we bent our way!   30

'What noisome thought could urge our parents so –
To leave the country and to London go!
The rural scene to change for houses, brown,
And barter health for the thick smoke of town!
What demon tempts him from our home to go
In horrid New Street to pour forth our woe? –
Oft – oft we've hoped this hour we ne'er might see,
Yet London – now at last we come to thee!
Oh! why was New Street so attractive made, –
Or why our Dad so easily betrayed?
Why heed we not as swift we ride along
The farewell peal of Highgate bells ding dong, –
Or wherefore think the flowery hedges hide, –
The grunting pigs, and fowls in speckled pride?
Why think we these less pleasing to behold
Than dirty streets which lead to houses old!
Sad was the hour and luckless was the day
When first from Bowman's Lodge we bent our way!

'Oh! cease our fears! all grumbling as we go,
While thought creates unnumbered scenes of woe, –
What if the mobs in all their ire we meet!
Oft in the dust we trace their crowded feet, –
And fearful – oft when day's November light
Yields up her yellow reign to gas-lit night,
By mischief roused they scour the streets, and fly,
While radical reform is all they cry:
Before them Death with fire directs their way,
Fills the loud yell and guides them to their prey.
Sad was the hour and luckless was the day
When first from Bowman's Lodge we bent our way.

'At that dread hour the noise of fire shall sweep –
If aught of rest we find, upon our sleep,
Or some rude thief bounce through the window – smash –
And wake our dozings with a hideous crash,
Thrice happy they – the Catharine Street poor –
From wish of town – from dread of fire secure!

They tempt no New Street, and no thieves they find! –
No carts of goods have they – before – behind! –
Sad was the hour and luckless was the day   70
When first from Bowman's Lodge we bent our way!

'Oh! Hapless Lears! – for that your care hath won, –
The large sidegarden will be most undone! –
Big swelled our hearts, on this same mournful day
When low the plants drooped down – as thus they seemed
    to say; –
"Farewell! ye Lears whom fruits could not detain! –
Whom flowrets drooping buds implored in vain! –
Yet as ye go may every blow fall down,
Weak as those buds on each receiving crown, –
So may ye see nor care – nor grievous fuss, –   80
Nor e're be cast to earth – to die like us! –"
Ah! might we safely to our home return –
Say to our garden – "Cease – no longer mourn! –"
Ah! might we teach our hearts to lose their fears,
And linger there our yet remaining years!'
They said – and ceased: lamenting o'er the day,
When first from Bowman's Lodge they bent their way.

To Miss Lear on her Birthday

Dear, and very dear relation,
Time, who flies without cessation, –
Who ne'er allows procrastination, –
Who never yields to recubation
Nor ever stops for respiration,
Has brought again in round rotation
The once a yearly celebration
Of the day of thy creation, –
When another augmentation
Of a whole year in numeration   10
Will be joined in annexation

To thy former glomeration
Of five seven-years' incalculation.
And in this very blest occasion
A thought has crossed my imagination,
That I 'neath an obligation
To make to thee a presentation,
(So 'tis the custom of our nation)
Of any trifling small donation,
Just to express my gratulation
Because of thy safe peragration
To one more long year's termination;
But having made an indagation
As to my moneyed situation,
(What must have been my indignation
Mortification, and vexation)
I tell you sans equivocation,
– I found – through dire depauperation,
A want of power – my sweet relation,
To practise my determination! –

So as the fates ordained frustration
I shortly ceased my lamentation
And, though it caused much improbation,
I set to work with resignation
To torture my imagination,
To spin some curious dication
To merit p'raps thine approbation, –
At least to meet thine acceptation,
And – after much deliberation
And 'mongst my thoughts much altercation,
I fixed that every termination
To every line should end in -ation! –
Now – since I've given this explanation,
Deign to receive my salutation
And let me breathe an aspiration
To thee – this day of thy creation.

First then, I wish thee, dear relation,
Many a sweet reduplication
Of this thy natal celebration:
And may'st thou from this first lunation   50
Unto thy vital termination
Be free from every derogation
By fell diseases' contamination,
Whose catalogic calculation
Completely thwarts enumeration, –
Emaciation, – fomentation,
With dementation – deplumation,
And many more in computation
For these are but an adumbration: –
– And may'st thou never have occasion   60
For any surgic operation
Or medical administration, –
Sanguification, – defalcation, –
Cauterization – amputation –
Rhabarbaration – scarification
And more of various designation: –
May'st thou be kept in preservation
From every sort of vitiation
By evil's dark depreciation: –
Intoxication – trucidation, –   70
From malversation – desecration –
From giving way to execration,
And every sinful machination: –
And in thy daily occupation –
Whether it be discalceation,
Or any other ministration
May'st thou not meet the least frustration;
May'st thou withstand all obtrectation
Thrown out to mar thy reputation; –
May'st thou be free from altercations   80
Or with thy word or thy relations; –
And (though it wants corroboration,
Yet not quite void of confirmation, –)
If as report gives intimation

You are about to change your station,
May every peaceful combination
Of bliss await your situation
In matrimonial elevation –
May'st thou be loved with veneration –
– By none be held in detestation, –
And towards thy life's advesperation,
When most are prone to [   ]
Their feeble limbs to desiccation, –
Their strength through years to deliquation, –
Their minds and brains to conquassation, –
Their failing speech to aberration, –
Their wearied taste to nauseation, –
                    then,
Then, may'st thou, – Oh dear relation,
Always receive refullerlation, –
Thy frame imbibe reanimation, –
Thy reason hold her wonted station
And keep her prudent scintillation,
Till thou descend'st by slow gradation
Unto thy final destination –
The long last home of all creation.
– This is my birthday aspiration; –
– Believe it, ever dear relation
Sincere without exaggeration –
In every individual ation! –
Sanguine – in each anticipation –
And kindly meant in perpetration.

Finis.

The Shady Side of Sunnyside

Woe worth the day when folly gave the signal
(Or rather Hymen) to old father Brignall,
To marry that same stupid 'Hurrum, – Scurrum',
Through whom we lost the sunny side of Durham!

That Sunnyside! how sweet it must have been!
My heart quite longs for such a lovely scene!
I think I see it now, – so wide and roomy, –
And then so brilliant always! – never gloomy! –

The sun that lighted up its eastern side,
Its beams upon the western multiplied, –   10
And gleamed at once o'er all its lakes and towers, –
Ah! at that rate, all Durham had been ours! –

– Had! – did I say? Alas – 'tis past recalling!
(Or else I'd spent a week or two in brawling)
No – no – don't fret – 'tis safe from every danger,
While in the awful clutches of the Grainger.

There's all their nasty children too, – before
We can get at it – each to have a paw
Upon that sweet – delightful sunny shore! –
– A breeding race – those Graingers! Known of yore!   20

Well, it's no use our thoughts to stew and ferret; –
'Figs on it' – I say – like Granny Skerritt; –
But when we *do* get into Durham's county, –
We'll pay those Grainger folks for all their bounty!

Yes – yes! so long o'er Sunnyside we've brooded, –
And our illustrious blood so long deluded, –
That when for that great rout we give the signals –
Oh! woe to Graingers [   ] and Brignalls! –

Journal
1829

November 2nd Monday evening – took my place –
Went to a dance at nine o'clock, –
Jigged all the colour out of my face
And reached my lodgings at crow of cock.

November 3rd Packed up my luggage till half past four,
Got up at six, and drank some tea,
And set off as cold as the frozen sea, –
Wished goodbye – took my hats and umbrella –
10   And shivered and shook to the White Horse cellar.
Sat on the top of the stage and four –
For Robinson half an hour or more, –
Rattled and rumbled down the Strand
Where the mudscrapers stood in a dingy band,
And rode away from London smoke,
Or ever the light of day had broke.
Chelsea and Fulham and Putney Bridge, –
And Kingston on Thames with its banks of sedge, –
Esher and Cobham, how cold they were! –
Oh! it was enough to make anyone swear!
20   – Thumped my feet till I made them ache, –
Took out provisions, a meal to make, –
Offered a sandwich, – (I had but three,) –
To my neighbour, who sat with a shaky knee,
'Sir' – said she with a glutinous grin,
'I'll thank you for *two*, as they seem but thin, –
And shall feel quite glad if you'll give one 'arter,
To this here young lady wot's my darter.' –
As good as her word was the brazen wretch,
Down went three sandwiches all at a stretch.
30   – Ripley – Guildford and Godalming too –
Whitley – Northchapel and Chittingfold gate –
Saw us looking as black and blue
As a spoonful of milk in an empty plate.

After the coach at Petworth ran –
(He and his wife,) a hugey man –
Quite as globose as a harvest moon,
Up he got, and 'twas B. Colhoun.
– Down Fittleworth Hill we made a dash,
And walked on foot up Bury Hill side, –
Half hot – half cold – like a luke-warm hash,   40
And as stiff as a lobster's claw – wot's tied.
Arundel town at length reached we,
As early as ten minutes after three.
Went to the Bank: found no one there –
Wanted a dinner – the cupboard was bare, –
Set off to Peppering – Cloky and I –
Over the hard chalk merrily –
Halfway there heard a horrible clack –
– Sister and nephews coming back –
Couldn't return with them – nonsense quite –   50
So posted away in the dusky light –
And five o'clock it might very well be,
Ere I caught a glimpse of the old elm tree,
And popped on my friends like a powder puff –
Ha – Ha – Ha – ! – it was merry enough!
Gobbled enough to choke Goliath –
Drank my tea – and sat by the fire;
Saw the baby – that unique child –
Who squeaked – and stared – and sniffed – and
   smiled; –
Then went to bed with a very good will   60
And fell asleep ere you'd swallow a pill.

November 4th   Wednesday, rose before the sun, –
And scrambled away o'er stile and gate, –
Left a note to say where I'd run, –
And got to Arundel – just at eight.
Breakfast over – up the hill,
With Sarah to Brookfield sallied forth,
White frost covering the country still, –
Just like a frozen syllabub froth:

70   Saw the children – ate some oys-
          ters – and went out to see the boys: –
          Found them performing sundry strides, –
          Some by skates and some by slides, –
          Went back, and fixed to come and stay
          On Sunday next, then came away.
          Found the wind blew vastly bitterly, –
          Called at Lyminster – John at home, –
          Looked at the plates of Roger's Italy, –
          Talked of reform and Chancellor Brougham: –
80   Back to Arundel made a run, –
          And finished a lunch at half past one:
          Out again – and called at Tower
          House, and staid for half an hour.
          Walked again with Sister Sarah,
          Through roads which surely never looked barer, –
          Woods of gloomy and leafless trees,
          All in a state of shiver and freeze:
          Into the town again and dressed, –
          Devoured a dinner with infinite zest: –
90   Went with the Streets to tea next door, –
          Wardropers – Blanches and two or three more; –
          Played at Backgammon and Chess with James,
          – Got beaten, and gammoned at sundry games, –
          Eat stewed oysters at supper time, – read
          Original verses – and went to bed.

November 5th Thursday. Breakfasted. Cold again –
          Dismal and half inclined to rain, –
          Walked with Sarah to Hampton Beach, –
          Saw the sea twirl like a vomiting leech, –
100   Walked up and down by the grumbling tide
          Till our noses looked like Capsicums dried, –
          Half-past eleven – left behind,
          The soap-suddy waves, – and boisterous wind,
          – After demolishing buns and bread –
          And making our visages vulgarly red, –
          Called at Brookfield for half a minute,

But didn't go in – for no one was in it, –
Went to Calceto and stayed some time
With Mrs George – till one o'clock chime, –
Then home again – And calls of course –   110
And dined upon mutton and capers sauce.
After dinner – popped next door –
And sat a dozen minutes or more, –
Went into Uncle Richard's – at first, –
Just in order to see Miss Hurst, –
But found a lot of people there –
So stayed – to drive away toothache and care.
– Back then we went then – one and all,
And here Miss Bischoff had a fall.
And then we reached, as we'd designed –   120
Miss Upperton's – And then we dined, –
And lastly, setting off again,
Just as the day was on the wane,
We got to Arundel at last,
At five o'clock – or rather past.

And thus Ma'am, in these dogg'rel verses
All the remarkable reverses
Of fortune, which we met, as how –
Through our strange wanderings, you know –
Conclusion now – by saying that I   130
Can never forget them certainly, –
And hoping that your wine may be
As good to all infinity
Of time, and that your pears mayn't spoil, –
But multiply – like Widow's oil –
I have the pleasure to sign here,
Myself – Yours most obliged –
                                        E. Lear.

Turkey Discipline
(adapted to the tune of 'Shades of Evening')

Horrid Turkeys! what a pother!
Leave my Mother's gulls alone!
We, alas! can get no other,
If those precious two are gone! –
Still you persevere! – You Monsters! –
Over you have come – pell-mell! –
Oh! my gulls! – if you come near them
I will utter such a yell!!!

'Bless my heart – nine monstrous turkeys! –
Gracious! – all the garden's full! –
And one great one with a jerk has
Pounced upon my favourite gull!'
– Through the noise of turkeys calling,
Now was heard, distinct and well,
From the Southern window squalling
Many a long and awful yell.

Down rushed Fanny and Eliza; –
– Screams and squeaks and yowlings shrill, –
– Gulls and turkeys with their cries a-
round them echoed o'er the hill: –
What would they not give to fetch them
Such a blow! – sad to tell –
As poor Fanny ran to catch them,
Evil turkeys – down she fell! –

'When the light dies away on a calm summer's eve'

When the light dies away on a calm summer's eve
And the sunbeams grow faint and more faint in the west,
How we love to look on, till the last trace they leave
Glows alone like a blush upon modesty's breast! –
Lonely streak! dearer far than the glories of day
Seems thy beauty – 'mid silence and shadow enshrined, –
More bright as its loneliness passes away –
And leaves twilight in desolate grandeur behind! –
So when grief has made lonely and blighted our lot,
And her icy cold chain o'er our spirits has cast,
Will not memory oft turn to some thrice hallowed spot,
That shines out like a star among years that are past?
Some dream that will wake in a desolate heart,
Every chord into music that long has been hushed,
Mournful echo! – soon still – for it tolls with a smart,
That the joys which first woke it, are long ago crushed!

10

'From the pale and the deep'

From the pale and the deep
  From the dark and bright –
From the violets that sleep –
  Away from light: –
From the lily that flashes
  At morn's glad call –
The bee gathers honey
  And sweets from all. –

There are hearts like bees
  In a world such as this,
That are given to please
  Through sorrow and bliss: –

10

Be the heaven of life
   As dark as it will –
Amid pleasure and strife
   They are smiling still.

They've a tear for the sad, –
   But there's balm in their sigh, –
And they laugh with the glad
20   In sunshine and joy: –
They give hope to the gloom
   Of the mourner's thrall –
Like the bee they find honey
   And sweets in all.

Peppering Roads

If you wish to see roads in perfection –
   A climax of cart-ruts and stones –
Or if you've the least predilection
   For breaking your neck or your bones, –
If descents and ascents are inviting, –
   If your ankles are strangers to sprains, –
If you'd ever a penchant for sliding, –
   Then, to Peppering go by all means! –

Take a coach some dark night in November,
10   A party of four within side –
Ah! I once had that jaunt, I remember,
   And really I pretty near died! –
First across to my neighbour I tumbled
   Then into the next lady's lap,
For at ev'ry fresh rut we were jumbled
   And jolted at ev'ry new gap! –

So that when we had finished our journey
   The coachman who opened the door
Found us tangled so very topturvy –
   We rolled out in one bundle, – all four.   20
And then we were so whisped together,
   Legs – dresses – caps – arms – blacks and whites,
That some minutes elapsed before ever
   They got us completely to rights! –

If you go in a gig, you are sure to
   Get lost in a mist on the hills, –
There's a gibbetted thief on a moor too,
   Your mem'ry with murder that fills. –
And besides, if you ride in what fashion
   You will – you are sure to get splashed,   30
Till you get quite incensed, in a passion,
   And peppery – like mutton that's hashed.

Or if, on some fine frosty morning,
   You make up your mind for a walk, –
Oh! ere such be your project – take warning,
   For sunbeams will liquify chalk! –
Step by step you get clogged so – for sartin,
   With chalk round your shoes like a rope, –
For to comfort – and eke Day and Martin! –
   You might as well walk upon soap! –   40

From one end of the walk to the other –
   It's one awful bootjack to feet –
One mighty pedestrial slither –
   For Christianlike progress unmeet! –
Oh! the Peppering roads! Sure 'tis fit there
   Should be some requital at last, –
So the inmates you find, when you get there,
   Amply pay you for all you have passed! –

Miss Fraser's Album

My Album's open; come and see; –
    What, won't you waste a thought on me?
Write but a word, a word or two,
    And make me love to think on you.

Give me of your esteem a sample;
    A line will be of price untold:
In gifts, the heart is all and ample,
    It makes them worth their weight in gold.

Here friends assemble, hand and heart,
    Whom life may sever, death may part,
Sweet be their deaths, their lives well spent,
    And this their friendship's merriment.

The lov'liest wreath that glows
    'Neath summer's hand entwining
A thousand flowerets shows
    In blinded beauty shining: –
The lowly bell – the blushing rose, –
    Their varied charms combining. –

And when the sunlight flies
    And day's hushed toils are ending –
The sounds of evening rise
    In mingled sweetness blending: –
And distant bells, and Zephyr's sighs
    To soothe, their joys are lending:

As round the flowing wreath
    Variety is smiling,
And o'er those sounds that breathe
    The silent air beguiling, –

10

20

Through ev'ry page of mine
　　Th'unfading wreath we're twining,
Variety's sweet charms will shine,
　　One blended whole combining. –

Ruins of the Temple of Jupiter Aegina, Greece

Many the feet that filled
　　Thy halls and marble stairs
When the sun was used to gild
　　Thy white-robed worshippers;
These were forms too bright and fair,
　　Who were kneeling at thy shrine,
For their souls to feel the snare
　　Of homage – false as thine: –
There were shouts of revelry
　　From thy mount rose high and long,　　10
And the dark and distant sea
　　Used to echo back the song! –
And the far off glorious clashing
　　Of thy cymbaled votary –
Came, through the soft air flashing,
　　Like the sounds of years gone by.
Aegina! – they are fled –
　　Thy fame hath perishèd! –

The moss is on thy walls –
　　Silence and deep despair; –　　20
And the ruin as it falls
　　Gives the only echo there:
Thy music is not heard, –
　　Thy high raised roof is gone, –
And the solitary bird
　　Sits on the topmost stone: –
There are sunbeams ling'ring still,
　　Through thy far white pillars seen

But they only seem to tell
    Of what thou once hast been! –
30
And oft in silence o'er thee,
    The dark cloud passes on –
And it sheds a deeper glory
    O'er thy wild oblivion! –
Aegina! – With the dead
    Thy fame hath perishèd! –

Type of thy parent clime! –
    In ages past away,
Greece was like thee sublime –
40
    Like thee was bright and gay! –
And on thy mount wert thou
    Shrined in thy orient sky,
A gem upon the brow
    Of her fair liberty! –
But Greece has fallen, like thee, –
    Desolate – wildly lone; –
Her sons – the brave and free,
    Forgotten and unknown: –
The echo of her fountains
50
    Seems her lost children's sigh, –
And on her lov'liest mountains
    Sits dark captivity! –
Aegina! – Greece! – the dead,
    And you have perishèd! –

The Bride's Farewell

Farewell Mother! tears are streaming
Down thy tender pallid cheek,
I, in gems and roses gleaming,
One eternal sunshine dreaming,
Scarce this sad farewell may speak.
Farewell Mother! now I leave thee,

And thy love unspeakable,
One to cherish – who may grieve me,
One to trust – who may deceive me,
Farewell Mother – fare thee well!   10

Farewell Father! thou art smiling,
Yet there's sadness on thy brow,
A mingled joy and languor wiling
All my heart from thee beguiling
Tenderness to which I go, –
Farewell Father thou didst bless me
Ere my lips thy name could tell,
He may wound – who should caress me
Who should solace – may distress me,
Father, guardian, – fare thee well!   20

Farewell Sister – thou are twining
Round me an affection deep,
Gazing on my garb so shining
Wishing joy, but ne'er divining
Why a blessèd bride should weep:
Farewell Sister – have we ever
Suffered wrath our breasts to swell,
Ere gave looks or words that sever?
Those who should be parted never,
Sister dearest – fare thee well.   30

Farewell Brother; thou art brushing
Gently off those tears of mine,
And the grief that fresh was gushing
Thy most holy kisses hushing,
Can I e'er meet love like thine?
Farewell, brave and gentle Brother
Those more dear than words can tell
Love me yet – although another
Claims Ianthe! Father, Mother,
All beloved ones, – Fare ye well!   40

Ruby –

Accidentally shot. November 23rd, 1829. –

Poor Ruby is dead! and before her no more
    From the hearth and the furze-bush the rabbit shall rise, –
For her barking is hushed and her bounding is o'er,
    And the birds will hop over the turf where she lies.

And the fire will shine down on the hearthrug at night,
    But poor Ruby will never repose there again, –
For her last sleep has closed up her eyelids, and light
    Will beam bright on her tomb to arouse her in vain.

To the churchyard no more when the service is done
10   She will hasten to welcome her master and friends, –
Nor again chase her tail round and round in her fun, –
    For with life – Ruby's joy and her liberty ends. –

Poor dog! though the hand which so fondly she loved
    Was the same which in death made her dark eye grow dim, –
Yet, had language been hers – she would e'en have approved
    Of a deed e'er so fatal – if coming from him!

They'll miss thee – poor Animal! gentle and true,
    In the field and the parlour, [in both thou didst shine!]
For 'mongst dogs thou wast good ... and of mortals, how few,
20   Can boast of a life half so faultless as thine! –

Thou wilt never come back! – Yet in some future day
    When the grass and the daisies have grown o'er thy head –
They will think of thee often at evening – and say
    When they look at thy hearthrug – 'Poor Ruby is dead!' –

Miss Maniac

Around my brain there is a chain, and o'er my fevered soul
A darkness like that solemn gloom which once through Egypt
stole;

Sometimes I feel, but know not why, a fire within me burn,
And visions fierce and terrible, pursue where'er I turn;

Then I forget that earth is earth, and that myself am life,
And nature seems to die away in darkness, hell and strife.

But when my phrenzied fit is o'er, a dreary hour comes on, –

A consciousness of unknown things, – of reason overthrown.

Cold runs my blood from vein to vein – all vacant is mine eye,
And in my ears a sound of death, and dread eternity!

Then one by one my thoughts return, and from my grated cell
I gaze upon the mountain fir, the steep and woody dell;

And as I listen to the stream that dashes far below,
I pine for freedom as a joy I never more can know.

Beyond those far blue hills, I feel, was once my home of bliss,
And there my father's cottage stood, – a roof more blest than
   this.

Ah! now I think I see them come, the forms I used to love,
And hear the evening shepherd bell sound sweetly through our
   grove. –

But they are gone! – all past away – they only flash like rays
Of morning o'er my memory – my young – my happy days! –

They said that I was lovely then – and wreathed with flowers my
  brow,

Oh! would my cheek had been as pale – my eye as dim as now! –

For love with all its pleasures came, but ah! its guilt came too,
And peace – fair twin to innocence, no more my bosom knew!

Oh – thou who falsely – darkly lured my frail fond heart astray,

Then left me like a broken flower, alone to waste away,

Where art thou now? doth ever thought, thy dark hour rush
across,

Of me, – forsaken – fallen me, – to goad thee with remorse? –

Or hast thou in the stream of life, 'mid scenes and forms more
sweet,

Forgot these tears that madd'ning mourn, my guilt and thy
deceit? –

30

Go – lull more hearts with hopes of bliss, undreaming of a
snare,

Till they awake to shame and feel – the pangs such bliss must bear.

Deceive! Deceive! – I loved thee once, therefore I will not
curse; –

But if my soul were bared to thee – Hell could not wish thee
 worse! –

Yet, if a heart, e'en hard as thine, could feel but *half* the pain
Which woman's wounded bosom feels – 'twould ne'er deceive
 again! –

Oh! when the bubble pleasure burst, how slowly time rolled
   by, –

My thoughts were grief – my looks were shame, – my every
   breath a sigh! –

Still – still I feel the scoffs of those who, with a cruel scorn,
Made doubly sad the memory of hours for ever gone, –   40

Go along do! you hussey! –

And still I hear my father's voice – as with a dreadful wrath

He cursed me with a bitter curse, and friendless drove me forth.

It was a cold and cheerless eve – and through the dark'ning sky
The wind swept past in hurried gusts, and shook the trees on
high; –

My child was in my arms – my own – how quietly it slept!

I longed for morn yet feared it, and I wandered on and wept,

Till, worn with sorrow and fatigue, careless I sate me down,

And felt how doubly keen it is to mourn – and mourn alone!

Cold – cold we were – oh never since such chilling grief has
    press'd

50 Upon my heart whose strings seemed burst – and frozen in my
    breast;

And o'er my soul, like demon forms, dark recollections came,
My sorrows and my sins and all my pleasures bought with
    shame, –

Till through my brain they racked like fire, and every vein
    waxed hot,
And in confused despair, awhile e'en sorrow seemed forgot: –

Strange feelings, such as none but maniacs ever know or feel,
Rushed indistinctly on my mind, and reason seemed to reel,

Till, lost in unknown agony, I laughed as if in mirth,
Or shudd'ring – welcomed back the gloom of hell begun on
earth:

Then madness first his scorching hand held o'er my withered
brain, –

60   Ah – ha! – it was a deadly touch – but it never cooled again! –

'I slept, and back to my early days'

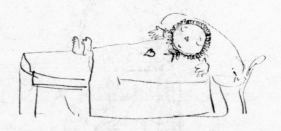

I slept, and back to my early days
Did wandering fancy roam –
When my heart vos light and my opes
    vos bright
And my own a appy ome.

When I dreamed I was young and hinnocent –
And my art vos free from care,
And my Parents smiled on their darling child,
And breathed for his [ ] a prayer.

Once again I was rising before the sun,
For in childhood I was told –
If its earliest ray on my head should play –
It would turn each tress to gold.

10

Once again I vos roaming through fields
    and flowers,
And I felt at each step new joys –
But I woke with a sigh that memory
Should revive what time destroys.

Resignation
'What must be must' or 'Baking Day'

I wish you would not mention it,
It gives me so much pain! –
Too soon by half I always know
'Tis baking day again! –
From pie to pie they hurry me, –
Loaves – tarts – preserves – and crusts –
And though I've not a moment's peace,
I cry – 'What must be, must!'

They bid me seek a change of fruit,
The charms which others see,   10
But – cherries – currants – plums – or pears –
They're all the same to me! –
'Tis true, I do not pluck the things,
Or clean 'em from the dust,
But though I don't – it's such a bore! –
Although 'What must be, must!'

They tell me pies are wanted now,
And eaten every day, –
They say they'll *always* have 'em too –
I only wish they may!   20
For my part, I'm so very sick
Of baking tarts and crust, –
I don't much think they'll catch me long,
To say – 'What must be, must!'

'I've just seen Mrs Hopkins – and read her the lines'

I've just seen Mrs Hopkins – and read her the lines,
(And they'll do for the mirror in print, she opines;) –
And so pray keep the book – till you've copied the rhyme,
For I shan't be in want of it now for some time.

I got home about five o'clock yesterday night –
As I fancy too you must have done – while 'twas light; –
For I saw you at Houghton – (I stood on the ridge
Upon Bury Hill side,) – and ride over the bridge.

I have sent you these numbers, by Robert – they'll be
An amusement perhaps to inspect after tea; –
They are beautiful things – and I think they're not dear
For both reading – and pictures. Good Bye. Edward Lear.

Ode to the little China Man

Who art thou – sweet little China Man? –
    Your name I want to know
With your lovely face so pale and wan –
    With a high diddle diddledy do. –

Your high cheek bones: – your screwed up mouth,
    How beautiful they be! –
And your eyes that ogle from north to south,
    With a high diddle diddledy dee! –

And your cultivated eyebrows too! –
    That depend from either eye! –
(I'm sure it's a fashion entirely new!) –
    With a high diddle diddledy di! –

But ev'ry one – (as the Frenchman said) –
    Ev'ry one to his way, –
(When he boiled in a pipkin his grandmother's head,) –
    With a high diddle diddledy da! –

Int'resting Mortal! – Whence art thou? –
    In figure surpassed by few! –
Tell us thy name – is it 'Chum-chu-wow'? –
    With a high diddle diddledy du? –

The little man fetched a sort of a sneer –
    As he made his sage reply –
While he twisted his eyebrow round his ear,
    With a high diddle diddledy dy. –

'Good folks' – (and he shook his noddle-ding-dong)
    'It's enough for you to know –
That in spite of my eyebrows – two feet long –
    I'm Miss Eliza's beau!!' –

Peppering Bell
On the marriage of Miss D—

At Burpham Church, the only bell
    The crazy tower can boast of
Is fractured like a walnut-shell
    Whose kernel's made the most of;
They thump its back, with many a whack,
    To set sweet tones a'flowing,
And each seventh day, the people say,
    'Hark! Hark! – the bell is going!'

But tired of such a horrid gong
   The Burphamites oft grumble,
'Why can't we have a good ding-dong, –
   And not that wretched dumb bell?'
Oh – be content with what heaven's sent,
   Nor be so very knowing –
For – Ah! – I fear, too soon you'll hear
   A better belle is going!

Letter to Harry Hinde

Dear Harry Hinde,
If you've a mind, –
This evening at eight,
Or hardly so late,
Being at leisure,
With very great pleasure,
I find I can come
To go with you home; –
(And drink of thy tea,
As I promised to thee:)
Yet – prithee don't, Harry,
By any means tarry
If this evening you should be
Engaged – for that would be
To me – the huge source
Of a deal of remorse;
For you know, if it won't suit,
I can bring up my flute
To skiggle and squeak
Any night of the week.
– Dask, now, I go to my dinner,
For all day I've been a-
way at the West End,
Painting the best end

Of some vast Parrots
As red as new carrots, –
(They are at the museum, –
– When you come you shall see 'em, –)
I do the head and neck first; –
– And ever since breakfast
I've had one bun merely!
So – yours quite sincerely
                    E.L.

30

Scrawl

Dear Ann –

I conjecture you'll like it no worse
If I write you this evening a letter in verse, –
But such an epistle as this, Ma'am, I tell ye – can't
Anyhow prove either pleasant or elegant, –
For writing by night – I am quite in a flurry
And nervously warm – like a dish of stewed curry.

I left Mrs Street upon yesterday morning,
(If my hand shakes – you'll know it's occasioned by
   yawning)
And really they used me the whole of the time
With such kindness – it can't be explained in a rhyme!
They stuffed me with puddings – chops – cutlets – and pies,
Wine and cakes (I was going to say up to my eyes
But I thought 'twas so vulgar it lacked this addition:
They crammed and they stuffed me, yea, unto repletion.)
Exceedingly careful were they of my health,
And I scarcely left home at all – saving by stealth;
– They never allowed me to walk by the river
For said they – 'Lest the fogs disagree with your liver! –'
And as for a stroll through a valley – "twere odds
If I went – that I didn't fall over the clods! – '
– 'Might I go and look over the Castle?' – 'Oh! Sidi
Mahommed!! – Suppose you should hap to grow giddy!
And pitch from the top over turrets and all –
Such a wap! breaking most of your bones in the fall! –'
So I stayed still at home and worked hard at my drawings,
And looked at the rooks – and sat hearing their cawings,
And walked out a little – a small pit-a-pat –
And endeavoured with heart and with soul to grow fat;
And indeed – just excepting – I sometimes am lame –
I don't seem in health or complexion the same; –
For my face has grown lately considerably fatter –

And has less the appearance of clarified batter
Than when, so malad, I left London turmoiled,
As pale as a sucking pig recently boiled.

Little Charles – I must say, seems improved on the whole –
But at books he's extremely dull – poor little soul! –
But the other child – Freddie – is noon night and morn
The most horrid young monkey that ever was born –
Such violent passions and tears in an ocean,
He kept the whole house in a constant commotion.   40

I now am ensconced in my favourite abode –
Which is Peppering, you know – with its sprain-ancle road;
They are all just as kind as they ever have been –
And the fields are beginning to look very green.
I have never procured yet a teal or a widgeon
But am drawing a very magnificent pigeon.
And as for my visits I'm going for to eat o-
f a dinner today with my friends at Calceto;
I leave this here place upon Saturday next,
Or on Sunday (I'll try to remember the text! –)   50
And stay ...

Letter to Fanny Jane Dolly Coombe

My dear Niece – par adoption –
   I shall not apologize for my departure from established rules so far
as to write to one so very juvenile as yourself, – as, – from the unusual
precocity of talent which you exhibited when but 6 months old I have
every reason to conclude you are by this time able to read writing; –
neither shall I excuse myself for quoting a foreign tongue – since I have
little doubt but that if you can master English – you are equally au fait
at French; – nor shall I offer any extenuation for the bad formation of
my letters – for I write by Candlelight – & in a hurry. – My letter indeed
is addressed to you – solely from a staunch belief that your whole kin-   10
dred – friends – connexions – & acquaintances are dead & departed –

& that you, – being the youngest – are the most likely to have survived so general a wreck – thus my epistle will prove a species of dead letter – & should by rights have been preluded by a *dead*ication. Faint hopes – however sometimes reanimate my mentals, & should the sundry folks below mentioned be still on the earth – I should thank you to convey their several messages to each, – which indeed is my principal reason for troubling you with so many skewers & pothooks. If you cannot yet speak your ideas – my love – you can squeak them you know.

Tell your Aunt Eliza – that on the evening before she left London – I was taken ill – with my old complaint in the head – so much so as to be unable to walk home – which consequently prevented me from meeting her at the Coach on the following morning. By a singular fatality – also – her tortoise died the next day. Thank my friend – your uncle Robert – for his recent letter – dated March 27th! – Tell him also – that when I ask for beasts or birds – it is only because I feel more pleasure in drawing from those given me by my intimate friends – than I could do from those otherwise come by – not from my being unable to get at specimens. – Having a rather Zoological connexion – & being about to publish British Quadrupeds – I have now living – 2 Hedgehogs, all the sorts of mice – weasels – Bats &c – & every beast requisite except a Pine Marten, – all of which, my dear child – I should be glad to present you with – did I suppose you could make the slightest use of them whatever.

Present my profound respects – to Mr W. Wardroper Esquire – with my best thanks for his friendly communications. I am glad that his Pamphlet – 'on curing Dropsy in Gallinaceous animals,' – has so extensive a sale. Pray – my dear – tell the 2 above mentioned friends never to incommode themselves in the least about writing to me, as they are aware how obtuse my feelings are, & that I bear being forgotten with much nonchalance.

Congratulate with Mrs Street from me, – on her recovery from her fall into the mill-pond – & from the 18 Paralytic strokes with which she was subsequently attacked: – my sister Ann is much gratified with her frequent correspondence in spite of her infirmities. – Should you see John Sayres – beg as a favour that he will not so continually torment me with graphic attentions.

Tell your papa – that I have been to the Opera & have heard Paganini – both of which pleasures have greatly contributed to widen the crack which nature had originally made in my brain.

Give my kindest regards & best respects to your Grandpapa and
Grandmama – Father & Mother – Uncle George – and Aunt Eliza –
who are not correspondents of mine – ask any body to kiss you from
me – & believe me – My dear Dolly –

> Your 3 parts crazy – & wholly affectionate
> Uncle Edward.

'Oh! Pan!'

> Oh! Pan!
> You dear old man! –
> Pray let us into your grotto, –
> It is so extremely hot oh!
> We've been at the *Pantheon*
> A'seeing all as to be seen –
> And now we're all tired and pale
> And afraid of a *coup de soleil.*
> So open your grotto –
> It is so dreadfully hottoh!
> Pan – Pan – darling old man!

10

Letter to George Coombe

My dear George – I'm convinced I am thoroughly cracked; –
I've waited a week e're your parcel I packed
In order to send it down free of post, yester=
=day, – by the hands of my Argyllshire sister, –
To save you an eightpence, – & all this is one of my
Violent fits of unusual economy: –
Mr Curtis's note you must know after all
Was the primary cause of my sending at all. –
So what was my horror in reaching today
In my bookcase – to find an aperient pill –
Which there has been thrust for these three weeks away –
To find the said note lying staring there still!
I declare I'd as soon have mounted a dragon! I
Felt quite dismayed with an impromptu agony. –
So now, – after thinking and reasoning and posing
I've made up my mind to the act of enclosing –
The entomological gentleman's letter, –
With a hope that my memory may shortly grow better.

Please the pigs! – Well, to call a new topic; – today,
I've seen *Miss* and Miss *Marg*aret *Wat*kins; they stay
Number 9 – Woburn Place – but that's nothing to you –
Though it fills very nicely a distich or two: –
Miss Margaret Watkins was dressed in pea-green –
As fine a young lady as never was seen; –
And I never remember – (except a great Dutchman
Who at Rotterdam sat at [the] end of a barge –
You might travel through Europe, yet scarcely see such man,)
– To have seen any creature one quarter so large. –

James Winkworth – Esq. – of the Royal Berks Corps –
Rides often by here – on a long-tailed grey horse –
And for fun – I should make such another bad rhyme, –
I'll conclude – and I dare say you'll think it's high time. –

Remember me pray to all yours – and the dear
Little dotties, – write soon – ever yours,

    Edward Lear

The Nervous Family

We're all nervous, very very nervous,
And we're all nervous at our house in town,
There's myself, and my Aunt, and my Sister, and my Mother, –
And if left in the dark we're all quite frightened at each other!
Our Dog runs away if there's a stranger in the house,
And our great Tabby Cat is quite frightened at a mouse, –
        For she's *so* nervous, very very nervous,
        And we're *all* nervous at our house in Town.

My poor shaking Aunt can't work at her needle,
And my shaking hand spills half my cup of tea –   10
When wine at her dinner my timid Sister's taking –
She drops it on the table, so much her hand is shaking –
And my poor old shaky Mother, when to take her snuff she tries
To pop it in her nose, – o! she pops it in her eyes.
        For she's so nervous, very very nervous,
        And we're *all* nervous at our house in Town.

We all at dinner, shake – shake at carving,
And as for snuffing candles, we all put out the light;
T'other evening after dinner we all to snuff did try,
But my Aunt couldn't do it, nor my Sister, nor could I;   20
'Child! Give *me* the snuffers!' – said my mother in a flout –
'*I'll* show you how to do it!' – so she did, and snuffed it *out*,
        For she's so nervous, very very nervous, –
        And we're all of us nervous at our house in Town.

Thus far is part of an old published song. – the rest is mine. EL.

We're getting much too nervous to go out to dinner
For we all sit a'shaking, just like puppets upon wires.
I'm too nervous to speak loud, so I'm scarcely ever able
To ask for what I want, or to talk across the table; –
And my poor shaking Aunt wheree're she sits, is sure to see,
Some sympathising Jelly always shaking vis à vis, –
      Which makes her *more* nervous, very very nervous, –
      And we're all of us nervous at our house in Town.

We're too nervous to get ready in time to go to church,
So we never go at all, since we once went late one day;
For the Clergyman looked *at* us, with a dreadful sort of frown,
And my poor shaky Mother caught his eye and tumbled down;–
And my Aunt and Sister fainted, – and tho' with care and pain
We dragged them slowly out, – yet we've never been again –
      And we're all nervous, very very nervous,
      And we're all of us nervous at our house in Town.

Our nerves in stormy weather are particularly *bad*,
And a single peal of thunder is enough to drive us *mad*.
So, when a storm comes on, we in a fright begin
To lock ourselves in closets where the lightning can't come in.
And for fear a little thunder to our nervous ears should come,
We each turn a barrel organ, and my Mother beats a drum,
      For we're all nervous, very very nervous,
      And we're all nervous at our house in Town.

The Nervous Family
Alternative version

My Aunt said I must marry, since there was none but I,
And the family would all be lost, if I should chance to die,
      And we're all &c.

So we talked it o'er and o'er, but what with cons and pros,
It was long before we settled to whom I should propose.
    For we're all &c.

At last it was decided, and trembling off I set,
And I learnt my speech by heart, for fear I should forget,
    For we're all &c.

I found she was alone, but when we were together,
I considered what to talk about, and hit upon the weather,
    For we're all &c.

I thought of my proposal, but that I'd quite forgot;
And could only mumble out, 'Don't you think it very hot?'
    For we're all &c.

I twiddled with my thumbs, and I look'd upon the floor;
And the Lady look'd at me, which made me *shakier* than
      before,
    For we're all &c.

So I fairly ran away, for I could not stammer out,
And she never could discover what the deuce I came about,
    For we're all &c.

And having failed the first time, for fear of being derided,
I shall never try again – or at least I'm not decided,
    For we're all &c.

'The gloom that winter casts'

The gloom that winter casts
    How soon the heart forgets –
When summer brings at last –
    The sun that never sets.
So love – when hope first gleams
    Forgets its former pain –
Amidst those sunny beams
    Which ne'er shall set again.

'My dear Mrs Gale – from my leaving the cradle'

My dear Mrs Gale – from my leaving the cradle
    Till now I have never such agony known,
What use *is* a Punch bowl without any ladle, –
    Be it Ivory – Silver – Wood – China – or bone? –

My Landlady rushes and foams in a flurry –
    Her Ladles for Punch and her Ladles for Soup,
Besides all her Ladles for Butter and Curry,
    She vows are all – 'smished' in one family Group!

Then dear Mrs Gale – have a little compassion
    If it's only a Ladle full – send me in one! –
And I'll ever proclaim you in my estimation –
    The most '*Ladle-like*' personage under the sun! –

Portraites of the inditchenous beestes of New Olland

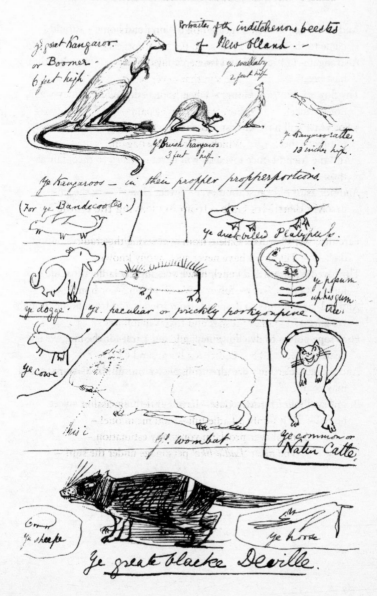

'My Sweet Home is no longer mine'

And Ah! when life's summer is flown – my fond home – should I
    come to thee then –
A stranger – unfriended and lone – couldst thou be to me what thou
    hast been!
Thy flowers may still bloom – but in vain; – thy tall elms may wave,
    not for me; –
– For years will have broken the chain, which hath bound me so
    fondly to thee,
– And the friend I once loved so will never – return to thee, fair as
    thou art,
And not as of old canst thou ever – Sweet Home! – soothe this
    desolate heart! –

Fare thee well! I will never forget – the scenes of my youth's happy
    day: –
Thy loved haunts will dwell with me yet, and cheer me thro' life's
    lonely way.
And ah! 'tis not ours to despond, from friends and from home though
    we part –
For Hope points to dwellings beyond, and a rest for the lone weary
    heart. –
And though, e'er life's day-dream shall close, amid far distant scenes I
    may roam, –
Bright symbol of future repose, – I will ever think of thee sweet
    home! –

[Illustrations for 'Kathleen O'More']

My Love still I think that I see her once more – But alas! She has left
me below to deplore – My own little Kathleen – My poor little
Kathleen – my Kathleen O'More

Her hair glossy black her eyes were of blue – Her color still changing
– her smile ever new – so pretty was Kathleen, &c &c &c &c –

She milked the dun cow – which ne'er offered to stir, Tho wicked it was it was gentle to her – so kind was my Kathleen – &c &c &c &c &c

She sat by the Door one cold afternoon – To hear the wind blow, & to look at the Moon – so pensive was Kathleen &c &c &c

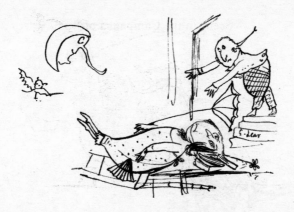

Cold was the night breeze as blow'd round her door. It *killed* my poor
   Kathleen she drooped from that hour – & I lost my poor Kathleen
   – &c &c &c

The bird of all birds as I loves the best Is the robin as builds in the
   Churchyard her nest, for he seems to watch Kathleen – *hop* lightly
   on Kathleen &c &c &c

Scene in the Campagna of Rome

[Lear's adventures on horseback]

1. L[ear] & K[night] leave Frascati – July 28th 1842. – Villa Taverna.

L. contemplates a ferocious horse with feelings of distrust.

2. Frascati. V. Taverna.

L. declares that he considers his horse far from tame.

3. Frascati. V. Taverna.

L. casually seats himself on the wrong side of his saddle.

4. V. Taverna. Frascati.

L. changes his position for the sake of variety.

5. V. Mondragone. Frascati.

L. perceives he has not seated himself properly.

6. K. & [L.] commence their journey.

L. is advised by K. to hold his reins short.

7. Frascati. Villa Mondragone.

L. is politely requested by K. to stop his horse.

8. M[onte] Porzio.

K. enquires amiably of L. if his stirrups are sufficiently short.

9. M. Porzio.

K. & L. are pursued by an irascible ox.

10. K. & L. pass M. Porzio & M. Compatri.

L. is requested by K. not to rise so exceedingly high from his saddle.

11. Monte Compatri.

L. descends an unsatisfactory hill in a pensive manner.

12. K. & L. pass Colonna.

L. is besought by K. to sit back on his saddle.

13. near Gallicano.

L. is immersed in an indefinite quagmire.

14. K. & L. arrive at Gallicano.

L. is informed by K. that he had better put his feet nearer to his horse's sides.

15. Ponte Lupo: – near Gallicano.

K. entreats L. to observe a large bridge called Ponte Loophole.

21. K. & L. proceed to Tivoli.

L. becomes suddenly and imperceptibly entangled in an obstructive Olive=tree.

23. K. & L. visit the temple by moonlight.

K. & L. discern a predominant Ghost.

25. Tivoli – K. & L. commence their journey back to Frascati.

L. is confidentially assured by the groom that he has mounted his horse incorrectly.

26. K. & L. pass through San Gregorio.

K. affectionately induces L. to perceive that a thornbush has attached itself to his repugnant horse.

27. K. & L. pass Casape & Poli, returning by Gallicano to Zagarolo.

L. is much disturbed by several large flies.

33. K. & L. proceed from Zagarolo to Frascati.

K. & L. are attacked by several very venomous Dogs in the vicinity of Colonna.

[Limericks for the 1846 and 1855 editions
of *A Book of Nonsense*]

There was an old Derry down Derry,
Who loved to see little folks merry;
   So he made them a Book,
   And with laughter they shook,
At the fun of that Derry down Derry!

There was an Old Man of Coblenz,
The length of whose legs was immense;
He went with one prance, from Turkey to France,
That surprising Old Man of Coblenz.

There was an Old Man of Peru,
Who watched his wife making a stew;
But once by mistake, in a stove she did bake,
That unfortunate Man of Peru.

There was an Old Man of the Hague,
Whose ideas were excessively vague;
He built a balloon, to examine the moon,
That deluded Old Man of the Hague.

There was an Old Man of Leghorn,
The smallest as ever was born;
But quickly snapped up he, was once by a puppy,
Who devoured that Old Man of Leghorn.

There was a Young Lady of Bute,
Who played on a silver-gilt flute;
She played several jigs, to her uncle's white pigs,
That amusing Young Lady of Bute.

There was an Old Man of Calcutta,
Who perpetually ate bread and butter;
Till a great bit of muffin, on which he was stuffing,
Choked that horrid Old Man of Calcutta.

There was an Old Person of Chester,
Whom several small children did pester;
They threw some large stones, which broke most of his bones,
And displeased that Old Person of Chester.

There was a Young Lady whose eyes,
Were unique as to colour and size;
When she opened them wide, people all turned aside,
And started away in surprise.

There was an Old Man of Kilkenny,
Who never had more than a penny;
He spent all that money, in onions and honey,
That wayward Old Man of Kilkenny.

There was an Old Man of Kamschatka,
Who possessed a remarkably fat cur;
His gait and his waddle, were held as a model,
To all the fat dogs in Kamschatka.

There was an Old Man of Columbia,
Who was thirsty, and called out for some beer;
But they brought it quite hot, in a small copper pot,
Which disgusted that Man of Columbia.

There was an Old Man of Berlin,
Whose form was uncommonly thin;
Till he once, by mistake, was mixed up in a cake,
So they baked that Old Man of Berlin.

There was an Old Person of Tartary,
Who divided his jugular artery;
But he screeched to his wife, and she said, 'Oh, my life!
Your death will be felt by all Tartary!'

There was an Old Man of the Cape,
Who possessed a large Barbary Ape;
Till the Ape one dark night, set the house on a light,
Which burned that Old Man of the Cape.

There was an Old Person of Burton,
Whose answers were rather uncertain;
When they said, 'How d'ye do?' he replied, 'Who are you?'
That distressing Old Person of Burton.

There was an Old Man of Vienna,
Who lived upon Tincture of Senna;
When that did not agree, he took Camomile Tea,
That nasty Old Man of Vienna.

There was an Old Man of th' Abruzzi,
So blind that he couldn't his foot see;
When they said, 'That's your toe,' he replied, 'Is it so?'
That doubtful Old Man of th' Abruzzi.

There was an Old Man of Corfu,
Who never knew what he should do;
So he rushed up and down, till the sun made him brown,
That bewildered Old Man of Corfu.

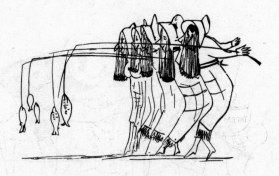

There was an Old Man of Marseilles,
Whose daughters wore bottle-green veils;
They caught several fish, which they put in a dish,
And sent to their Pa' at Marseilles.

There was an Old Man of Nepaul,
From his horse had a terrible fall;
But, though split quite in two, by some very strong glue,
They mended that Man of Nepaul.

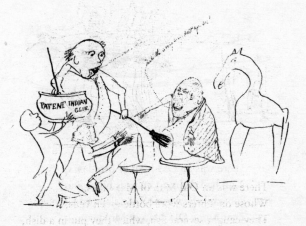

There was an Old Man of the Isles,
Whose face was pervaded with smiles;
He sung high dum diddle, and played on the fiddle,
That amiable Man of the Isles.

There was an Old Man of Moldavia,
Who had the most curious behaviour;
For while he was able, he slept on a table,
That funny Old Man of Moldavia.

There was an Old Man of Vesuvius,
Who studied the works of Vitruvius;
When the flames burnt his book, to drinking he took,
That morbid Old Man of Vesuvius.

There was a Young Lady of Tyre,
Who swept the loud chords of a lyre;
At the sound of each sweep, she enraptured the deep,
And enchanted the city of Tyre.

There was an Old Person of Rheims,
Who was troubled with horrible dreams;
So, to keep him awake, they fed him with cake,
Which amused that Old Person of Rheims.

There was a Young Lady of Hull,
Who was chased by a virulent Bull;
But she seized on a spade, and called out – 'Who's afraid!'
Which distracted that virulent Bull.

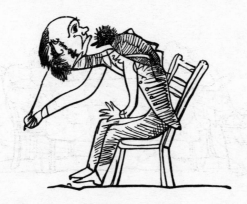

There was an Old Man of Quebec,
A beetle ran over his neck;
But he cried, 'With a needle, I'll slay you, O beadle!'
That angry Old Man of Quebec.

There was an Old Person of Gretna,
Who rushed down the crater of Etna;
When they said, 'Is it hot?' He replied, 'No, it's not!'
That mendacious Old Person of Gretna.

There was an Old Person of Prague,
Who was suddenly seized with the plague;
But they gave him some butter, which caused him to mutter,
And cured that Old Person of Prague.

There was an Old Man of the Dee,
Who was sadly annoyed by a flea;
When he said, 'I will scratch it' – they gave him a hatchet,
Which grieved that Old Man of the Dee.

There was an Old Man of the West,
Who wore a pale plum-coloured vest;
When they said, 'Does it fit?' he replied, 'Not a bit!'
That uneasy Old Man of the West.

There was an Old Man of Peru,
Who never knew what he should do;
So he tore off his hair, and behaved like a bear,
That intrinsic Old Man of Peru.

There was a Young Lady of Troy,
Whom several large flies did annoy;
Some she killed with a thump, some she drowned at the pump,
And some she took with her to Troy.

There was a Young Lady of Clare,
Who was sadly pursued by a bear;
When she found she was tired, she abruptly expired,
That unfortunate Lady of Clare.

There was a Young Lady of Norway,
Who casually sat in a doorway;
When the door squeezed her flat, she exclaimed, 'What of that?'
This courageous Young Lady of Norway.

There was a Young Lady of Sweden,
Who went by the slow train to Weedon;
When they cried, 'Weedon Station!' she made no observation,
But thought she should go back to Sweden.

There was an Old Man of the South,
Who had an immoderate mouth;
But in swallowing a dish, that was quite full of fish,
He was choked, that Old Man of the South.

There was an Old Person of Ischia,
Whose conduct grew friskier and friskier;
He danced hornpipes and jigs, and ate thousands of figs,
That lively Old Person of Ischia.

There was a Young Lady whose nose,
Was so long that it reached to her toes;
So she hired an Old Lady, whose conduct was steady,
To carry that wonderful nose.

There was an Old Man of Madras,
Who rode on a cream-coloured ass;
But the length of its ears, so promoted his fears,
That it killed that Old Man of Madras.

There was an Old Lady whose folly,
Induced her to sit in a holly;
Whereon by a thorn, her dress being torn,
She quickly became melancholy.

There was an Old Man of the Coast,
Who placidly sat on a post;
But when it was cold, he relinquished his hold,
And called for some hot buttered toast.

There was an Old Person of Troy,
Whose drink was warm brandy and soy;
Which he took with a spoon, by the light of the moon,
In sight of the city of Troy.

There was an Old Person of Buda,
Whose conduct grew ruder and ruder;
Till at last, with a hammer, they silenced his clamour,
By smashing that Person of Buda.

There was an Old Person of Sparta,
Who had twenty-five sons and one daughter;
He fed them on snails, and weighed them in scales,
That wonderful Person of Sparta.

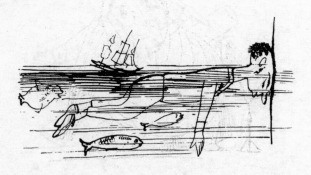

There was an Old Sailor of Compton,
Whose vessel a rock it once bump'd on;
The shock was so great, that it damaged the pate
Of that singular Sailor of Compton.

There was an Old Man of Apulia,
Whose conduct was very peculiar;
He fed twenty sons, upon nothing but buns,
That whimsical Man of Apulia.

There was an Old Person of Hurst,
Who drank when he was not athirst;
When they said, 'You'll grow fatter,' he answered, 'What matter?'
That globular Person of Hurst.

There was a Young Lady of Turkey,
Who wept when the weather was murky;
When the day turned out fine, she ceased to repine,
That capricious Young Lady of Turkey.

There was a Young Lady of Dorking,
Who bought a large bonnet for walking;
But its colour and size, so bedazzled her eyes,
That she very soon went back to Dorking.

There was an Old Person of Rhodes,
Who strongly objected to toads;
He paid several cousins, to catch them by dozens,
That futile Old Person of Rhodes.

There was an Old Man of Cape Horn,
Who wished he had never been born;
So he sat on a chair, till he died of despair,
That dolorous Man of Cape Horn.

There was an Old Man of Jamaica,
Who suddenly married a Quaker!
But she cried out – 'O lack! I have married a black!'
Which distressed that Old Man of Jamaica.

There was an Old Man of the West,
Who never could get any rest;
So they set him to spin, on his nose and his chin,
Which cured that Old Man of the West.

There was an Old Man of the East,
Who gave all his children a feast;
But they all ate so much, and their conduct was such,
That it killed that Old Man of the East.

There was a Young Lady of Poole,
Whose soup was excessively cool;
So she put it to boil, by the aid of some oil,
That ingenious Young Lady of Poole.

There was an Old Man of Dundee,
Who frequented the top of a tree;
When disturbed by the crows, he abruptly arose,
And exclaimed, 'I'll return to Dundee.'

There was an Old Man of New York,
Who murdered himself with a fork;
But nobody cried though he very soon died, –
For that silly Old Man of New York.

There was an Old Man of the North,
Who fell into a basin of broth;
But a laudable cook, fished him out with a hook,
Which saved that Old Man of the North.

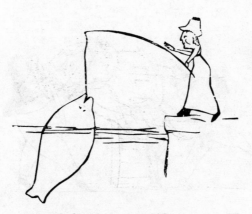

There was a Young Lady of Wales,
Who caught a large fish without scales;
When she lifted her hook, she exclaimed, 'Only look!'
That extatic Young Lady of Wales.

There was an Old Man of the Nile,
Who sharpened his nails with a file;
Till he cut off his thumbs, and said calmly, 'This comes –
Of sharpening one's nails with a file!'

There was an Old Man of Bohemia,
Whose daughter was christened Euphemia;
Till one day, to his grief, she married a thief,
Which grieved that Old Man of Bohemia.

There was an Old Man of the Wrekin,
Whose shoes made a horrible creaking;
But they said 'Tell us whether, your shoes are of leather,
Or of what, you Old Man of the Wrekin?'

There was an Old Person of Cheadle,
Was put in the stocks by the beadle;
For stealing some pigs, some coats, and some wigs,
That horrible Person of Cheadle.

There was an Old Person of Ems,
Who casually fell in the Thames;
And when he was found, they said he was drowned,
That unlucky Old Person of Ems.

There was a Young Lady of Welling,
Whose praise all the world was a telling;
She played on the harp, and caught several carp,
That accomplished Young Lady of Welling.

There was an Old Lady of Prague,
Whose language was horribly vague;
When they said, 'Are these caps?' she answered, 'Perhaps!'
That oracular Lady of Prague.

There was an Old Person of Cadiz,
Who was always polite to all ladies;
But in handing his daughter, he fell into the water,
Which drowned that Old Person of Cadiz.

There was a Young Lady of Russia,
Who screamed so that no one could hush her;
Her screams were extreme, no one heard such a scream,
As was screamed by that Lady of Russia.

There was a Young Lady of Parma,
Whose conduct grew calmer and calmer;
When they said, 'Are you dumb?' she merely said, 'Hum!'
That provoking Young Lady of Parma.

There was a Young Girl of Majorca,
Whose aunt was a very fast walker;
She walked seventy miles, and leaped fifteen stiles,
Which astonished that Girl of Majorca.

There was an Old Man of Kildare,
Who climbed into a very high chair;
When he said, – 'Here I stays, – till the end of my days,'
That immovable Man of Kildare.

[Other early limericks]

There was an old man who forgot,
That his tea was excessively hot;
When they said 'Let it cool' – He answered 'You fool!
I shall pour it back into the pot.' –

There was an old man of Orleans,
Who was given to eating of beans;
Till once out of sport, he swallowed a quart,
That dyspeptic old man of Orleans.

There was an old man of the Dee,
Who always was partial to tea;
Buttered toast he abhorred, and by muffins was bored,
That uncommon old man of the Dee.

There was an old person of Leith,
Who had the most dolorous teeth;
So she had a new set. 'I'll eat quantities yet,'
Said that fortunate woman of Leith.

There was an old person whose legs,
Bore a striking resemblance to pegs;
When they said, 'Can you toddle?' he answered – 'I waddle,
What else *should* I do with my legs?'

There was an old man whose delight,
Was to play on the trumpet all night;
When they said, 'You're a bore!' he answered, 'What for?
Mayn't I play on the trumpet all night?'

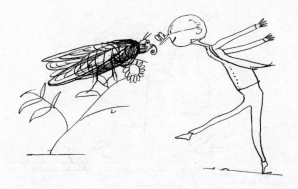

There was an old man who said, 'See!
I have found a most beautiful bee!'
When they said, 'Does it buzz?' he answered, 'It *does*,
I never beheld such a bee!'

There was an old man of Lodore,
Who heard the loud waterfall roar;
But in going to look, he fell into a brook,
And he never was heard of no more.

There was an old person so silly,
He poked his head into a lily;
But six bees who lived there, filled him full of despair,
For they stung that old person so silly.

There was an old man whose repose,
Consisted in warming his toes;
When they said, 'Are they done?' he answered, 'What fun!
Do you think I'm a'cooking my toes?'

There was an old man whose despair,
Induced him to purchase a bear;
He played on some trumpets, and fed upon crumpets,
Which rather assuaged his despair.

There was an old person of Sidon,
Who bought a small pony to ride on;
But he found him too small to leap over a wall,
So he walked, that old person of Sidon.

There was an old person whose mirth,
Induced him to leap from the earth;
But in leaping too quick, he exclaimed, 'I'm too sick
To leap any more from the earth.'

There was an old lady of Leeds,
Who was always a'doing good deeds;
She sate on some rocks with her feet in a box,
And her neck was surrounded by beads.

There was an old man in a boat,
Who complained of a pain in his throat;
When they said, 'Can you screech?' he replied, 'I beseech
You won't make any noise in my boat!'

There was an old man whose desire,
Was to sit with his feet in the fire;
When they said, 'Are they 'ot?', he replied, 'No, they're not!
You must put some more coals on the fire.'

There was an old person of Calais,
Who lived in a blue marble palace;
But on coming downstairs, he encountered some bears,
Who swallowed that person of Calais.

There was an old man with a light,
Who was dressed in a garment of white;
He held a small candle, with never a handle,
And danced all the merry long night.

There was an old man who said 'O! –
Let us come where the humble bees grow!
There are no less than five sitting still on a hive,
Singing songs to their children below.'

There was an old man who made bold,
To affirm that the weather was cold;
So he ran up and down, in his grandmother's gown,
Which was woollen, and not very old.

There was an old man whose Giardino
Produced only one little bean o!
When he said – 'That's enough!' – They answered,
    'What stuff!
You never can live on *one* bean o!'

There was an old man whose Giardino
Was always so cheerful and green O –
Every hour he could spare, – He sate in a chair
In the midst of his summer Giardino.

There was an old person of Sheen,
Whose carriage was painted pea=green;
But once in the snow the horse would not go,
Which disgusted that person of Sheen.

There was an old person of Shields,
Who rambled about in the fields;
But, being infirm, he fell over a worm
And sighed that he'd ever left Shields.

There was an old person whose tears
Fell fast for a series of years;
He sat on a rug, and wept into a jug
Which he very soon filled full of tears.

The Hens of Oripò

The agèd hens of Oripò,
   They tempt the stormy sea;
Black, white and brown, they spread their wings,
   And o'er the waters flee;
And when a little fish they clutch
   Athwart the wave so blue,
They utter forth a joyful note, –
   A cock-a-doodle-doo!
O! Oo! Oripò – Oo! the hens of Oripò!

The crafty hens of Oripò,
   They wander on the shore,
Where shrimps and winkles pick they up,
   And carry home a store;

For barley, oats, or golden corn,
   To eat they never wish,
All vegetably food they scorn,
   And only seek for fish.
O! Oo! Oripò – Oo! the hens of Oripò!

The wily hens of Oripò,
   Black, white and brown and gray,
They don't behave like other hens;
   In any decent way.
They lay their eggs among the rocks,
   Instead of in the straw,
. . . .
. . . .
O! Oo! Oripò – Oo! the hens of Oripò!

The nasty hens of Oripò,
   With ill-conditioned zeal,
All fish defunct they gobble up,
   At morn or evening meal.
Whereby their eggs, as now we find,
. . . .
A fishlike ancient smell and taste
   Unpleasant doth pervade.
O! Oo! Oripò – Oo! the hens of Oripò!

'A was an Ant'

A

A was an Ant
Who seldom stood still,
And he made a small house
On the side of a hill.
a!
Little brown ant!

B

B was a Butterfly
Purple and green,
A more beautiful butterfly
Never was seen.
b!
Butterfly bright!

C

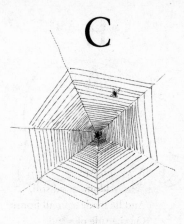

C was a Cobweb
Which caught a small fly,
Who tried to escape
From the spider so sly.
c!
Cobweb and Fly!

D

D was a Duck
With spots on his back,
Who lived in the water
And sometimes said Quack!
d!
Dear little duck!

E

E was an Elephant
Vast as to size,
With tusks and a trunk
And two small squinny eyes!
e!
Elephant's eyes!

F

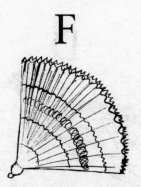

F was a Fan
Which was purple and green,
The most beautiful fan
That had ever been seen.
f!
Fine little fan!

G

G was a Goat
With a beautiful coat,
But his horns were too curly
Which made him quite surly.
g!
Cross little goat!

H

H was a Hat,
But the brim was too wide,
And the crown was too flat
And all of one side.
h!
What a bad hat!

I

I was some Ice
Which was awfully nice,
But which nobody tasted
And so it was wasted.
        i!
    Very cold ice!

J

J was some Jujubes
Exceedingly sweet,
And they were (by some persons)
Esteemed quite a treat.
        j!
    Sweet little jujubes!

K

K was a Kite
Which flew up on high,
All over the houses
And into the sky.
k!
Fly away kite!

L

L was a Lamp
So beauteous and bright,
Which illumined a room
On a very dark night.
l!
Luminous lamp!

M

M was a Mouse
With a very long tail,
But he never went out
In the rain or the hail.
m!
Poor little mouse!

N

N were some Nuts
Which were perfectly brown,
And being quite ripe
They all tumbled down.
n!
Tumble down nuts!

O

O was an Owl
Who objected to light
When he made a great noise
Every hour in the night.
o!
Noisy old owl!

P

P was a Pudding
As round as the moon,
And when it was cut
It was helped with a spoon.
p!
Elegant pudding!

Q

Q was a Quail
With a very short tail,
Having fed upon corn
Ever since he was born.
q!
Queer little quail!

R

R was a Rabbit
Who had a bad habit
Of nibbling the flowers
In the gardens and bowers.
r!
Naughty old rabbit!

S

S was a spoon
Which I certainly think
Was placed in some tea
To assist you to drink.
s!
Silvery spoon!

T

T was a Top
Which turned round and round,
And fell to the ground
With a musical sound.
t!
Turn about top!

U

U was an Urn
With hot water in it,
To bubble and burn
And make tea in a minute.
u!
Useful old urn!

V

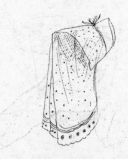

V was a Veil
With pink spots upon it,
Tied round with a string
Round a bottle green bonnet.
v!
Very fine veil!

W

W was a Whale
With a dreadful long tail,
Who rushed all so frantic
Across the Atlantic.
w!
Roll about whale!

X

X was King Xerxes
Who more than all Turks is
Renowned for his fashion
Of screaming with passion.
x!
Shocking old Xerxes!

Y

Y was a Yew
Which flourished and grew
By a lovely abode
Quite close to the road.
y!
Dark little yew!

Z

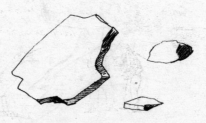

Z was some Zinc
Which caused you to wink
When you saw it so bright
In the summer sunlight.
z!
Pretty bright zinc!

'Ribands and pigs'

Ribands & pigs,
Helmets & Figs,
Set him a jigging & see how he jigs.

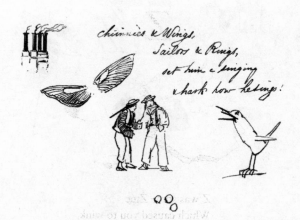

Chimnies & Wings,
Sailors & Rings,
Set him a singing & hark how he sings!

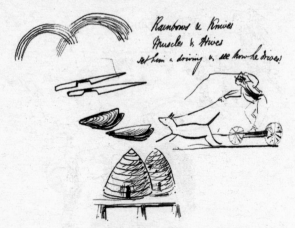

Rainbows & Knives
Muscles & Hives
Set him a driving & see how he drives!

Houses & Kings
Whiskers & Swings
Set him a stinging & see how he stings –

Herons & Sweeps
Turbans & Sheeps,
Set him a weeping & see how he weeps

Eagles & pears,
Slippers & Bears,
Set him a staring & see how he stares!

Tadpoles & Tops,
Teacups & Mops,
Set him a hopping & see how he hops!

20

Tadpoles & Tops,
Teacups & Mops,
Set him a hopping & see how he hops!

Teapots, & Quails,
Snuffers & snails,
Set him a sailing
& see how he sails!

Teapots, & Quails,
Snuffers & snails,
Set him a sailing & see how he sails!

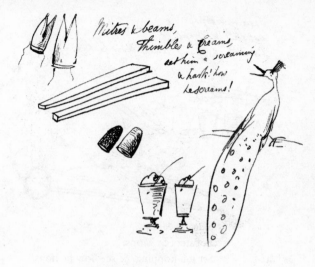

Mitres & beams,
Thimbles & Creams,
Set him a screaming & hark! how he screams!

Lobsters & owls,
Scissors and fowls,
Set him a howling & hark how he howls! –

30

Saucers & tops,
Lobsters & Mops,
Set it a hopping, & see how he hops!

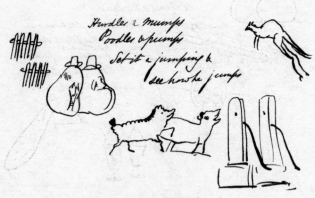

Hurdles & Mumps
Poodles & pumps
Set it a jumping & see how he jumps

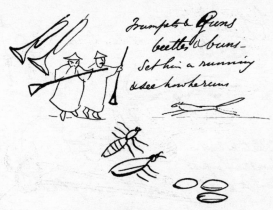

Trumpets & Guns
beetles & buns –
Set him a running & see how he runs

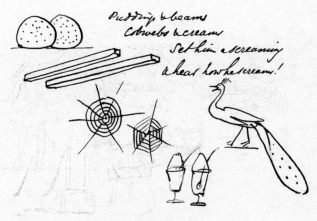

Puddings & beams
Cobwebs & creams
Set him a screaming & hear how he screams!

40

Cutlets & eyes –
Swallows & pies
Set it a flying & see how it flies

Watches & Oaks,
Custards & Cloaks
Set him a poking & see how he pokes

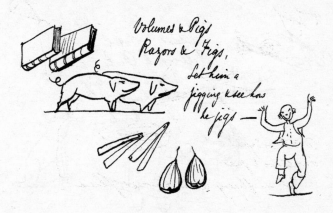

Volumes & Pigs
Razors & Figs,
Set him a jigging & see how he jigs –

50

Pancakes & Fins
Roses & Pins
Set him a grinning & see how he grins!

Scissors & Fowls,
Filberts & Owls
Set him a howling & see how he howls –

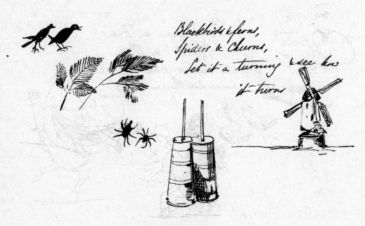

Blackbirds & ferns,
Spiders & Churns,
Set it a turning & see how it turns

Wafers & Bears,
Ladders & Squares,
Set him a staring & see how he stares!

Tea Urns & Pews,
Muscles & Jews,
Set him a mewing and hear how he mews –

Sofas & bees,
Camels & Keys
Set him a sneezing & see how he'll sneeze!

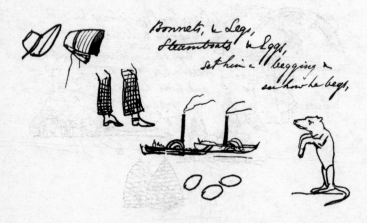

Bonnets, & Legs,
Steamboats & Eggs,
Set him a begging & see how he begs.

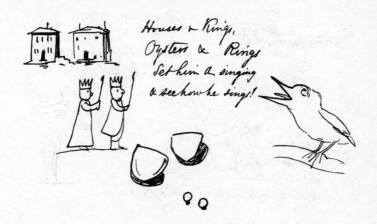

Houses & Kings,
Oysters & Rings
Set him a singing & see how he sings!

Rainbows & Wives
Puppies & Hives,
Set him a driving & see how he drives!

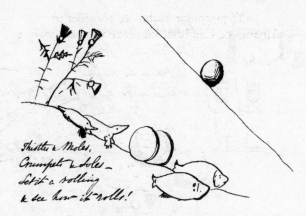

Thistles & Moles,
Crumpets & Soles –
Set it a rolling & see how it rolls!

80

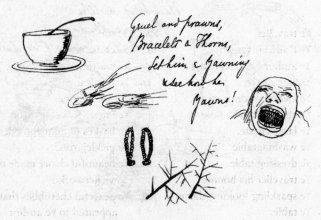

Gruel and prawns,
Bracelets & Thorns,
Set him a yawning & see how he yawns!

Ye poppular author & traveller in Albania & Calabrià, keepinge his feete warme

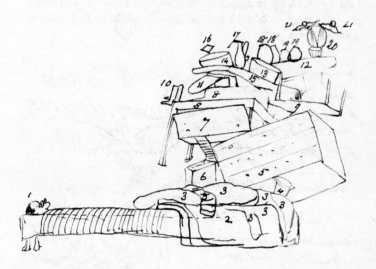

1. Ye traveller.
2. Ye Railwaie rugge.
3. Ye author his vestmentes.
4. his hatteboxe.
5. Ye Cheste of draweres
6. Ye chaire
7. Ye large cheste.
8. Ye washingtable
9. Ye dressing table.
10. Ye traveller his bootes.
11. Ye sparkling looking glasse.
12. Ye table.
13. Ye tinne tubbe
14. Ye china tub.
15. Ye matting rolled uppe.
16. Ye quadrangular pincushione.
17. Ye jugge.
18. Ye flaskes of gunnepowder.
19. Ye picklejarres.
20. Ye beautiful chaire made of wickerworke
21. Ye peaceful cherubbes that appeared to ye author when he fell asleepe.–

[Lear at the Royal Academy Schools]

I tried with 51 – little boys: – & 19 of us were admitted. And now I go with a large book and a piece of chalk to school every day like a good little boy. –

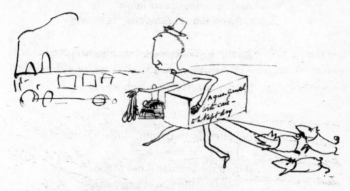

There was an old person of Ramleh,
Who purchased a little green Gamleh
As well as three pigs, some mice, and some figs,
All of which he took with him to Ramleh.

'O! Mimber for the County Louth'

O! Mimber for the County Louth
    Residing at Ardee!
Whom I, before I wander South,
    Partik'lar wish to see; –

I send you this – that you may know
    I've left the Sussex shore,
And coming here two days ago
    Do cough for evermore.

Or gasping hard for breath do sit
    Upon a brutal chair,
For to lie down in Asthma fit
    Is what I cannot bear.

    10

Or sometimes sneeze: and always blow
    My well-developed nose,

And altogether never know
    No comfort nor repose.

All through next week I shall be here,
    To work as best I may
On my last picture, which is near-
20   er finished every day.

But after the thirteenth, – (that's Sunday)
    I must – if able – start
(Or on the Tuesday if not Monday)
    For England's Northern part.

And thence I only come again
    Just to pack up and run,
Somewhere where life may less be pain,
    And somewhere where there's sun.

So then I hope to hear your ways
30   Are bent on English moves,
For that I trust once more to gaze
    Upon the friend I loves.

(Alas! Blue Posts I shall not dare
    To visit e're I go –
Being compulsed to take such care
    Of all the winds as blow.)

But if you are not coming now
    Just write a line to say so –
And I shall still consider how
40   Ajoskyboskybayso.

No more my pen: no more my ink:
    No more my rhyme is clear.
So I shall leave off here I think. –
        Yours ever,
                Edward Lear.

'Washing my rose-coloured flesh and brushing my beard with a hairbrush'

Dear F,

Washing my rose-coloured flesh and brushing my beard with a
    hairbrush, –
– Breakfast of tea, bread and butter, at nine o'clock in the morning,
Sending my carpetbag onward I reached the Twickenham station,
(Thanks to the civil domestics of good Lady Wald'grave's
    establishment,)
Just as the big buzzing brown booming bottlegreen bumblebizz boiler
Stood on the point of departing for Richmond and England's
    metropolis.

I say – (and if I ever said anything to the contrary I hereby retract it) –
I say – I took away altogether unconsciously your borrowed white
    filigree handkerchief;

After the lapse of a week I will surely return it,
And then you may either devour it, or keep it, or burn it, –   10
Just as you please. But remember I have not forgotten,
After the 26th day of the month of the present July,
That is the time I am booked for a visit to Nuneham.

Certain ideas have arisen and flourished within me,
As to a possible visit to Ireland, – but nobody
Comes to a positive certainty all in a hurry;
If you are free and in London, next week shall we dine at the *Blue*
    Posts?

Both Mrs Clive and her husband have written most kindly
Saying the picture delights them (the Dead Sea) extremely. –

20 Bother all painting! I wish I'd 200 per annum!
    – Wouldn't I sell all my colours and brushes and damnable messes!
    Over the world I would rove, North South East and *West* I would –
    Marrying a black girl at last, and slowly preparing to walk into
       Paradise!

    A week or a month hence, I will find time to make a queer Alphabet,
    All with the letters beversed and beaided with pictures,
    Which I shall give, (but don't tell him just yet,) to Charles Braham's
       little one.

    Just only look in the Times of today for accounts of the Lebanon!

    Now I must stop this jaw and write myself quite simultaneous,
    Yours with a l[ ] affection – the globular foolish Topographer.

                                                              E.L.

From a letter to George Grove

I hasten to inform you that in a wood very near here, there are Toad-stools of the loveliest and most surprising colour and form: – orbicular, cubicular and squambingular, and I even thought I perceived the very rare Pongchámbinnibóphilos Kakokreasópheros among others a few days back. You have therefore nothing better to do than to come with Penrose and hunt up and down St George's Hill for the better carrying out of the useful and beastly branch of science you have felt it your duty to follow. Provided also that you bring your own cooking utensils you may dine off your gatherings though I won't partake of the feast, my stomach being delicate.

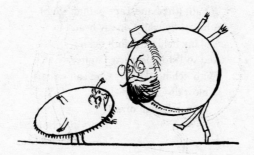

'But ah! (the Landscape painter said,)'

But ah! (the Landscape painter said,)
A brutal fly walks on my head
And my bald skin doth tickle;
And so I stop distracted quite,
(With itching skin for who can write?)
In most disgusting pickle –
   & merely sign myself

Yours affectionately
Edward Lear

[Additional limericks for the 1861 edition
of *A Book of Nonsense*]

There was an Old Man with a beard,
Who said, 'It is just as I feared! –
Two Owls and a Hen, four Larks and a Wren,
Have all built their nests in my beard!'

There was a Young Lady of Ryde,
Whose shoe-strings were seldom untied;
She purchased some clogs, and some small spotty dogs,
And frequently walked about Ryde.

There was an Old Man with a nose,
Who said, 'If you choose to suppose
That my nose is too long, you are certainly wrong!'
That remarkable Man with a nose.

There was an Old Man on a hill,
Who seldom, if ever, stood still;
He ran up and down, in his Grandmother's gown,
Which adorned that Old Man on a hill.

There was a Young Lady whose bonnet,
Came untied when the birds sate upon it;
But she said, 'I don't care! all the birds in the air
Are welcome to sit on my bonnet!

There was a Young Person of Smyrna,
Whose Grandmother threatened to burn her;
But she seized on the Cat, and said, 'Granny, burn that!
You incongruous Old Woman of Smyrna!'

There was an Old Person of Chili,
Whose conduct was painful and silly;
He sate on the stairs, eating apples and pears,
That imprudent Old Person of Chili.

There was an Old Man with a gong,
Who bumped at it all the day long;
But they called out, 'O law! you're a horrid old bore!'
So they smashed that Old Man with a gong.

There was an Old Lady of Chertsey,
Who made a remarkable curtsey;
She twirled round and round, till she sunk underground,
Which distressed all the people of Chertsey.

There was an Old Man in a tree,
Who was horribly bored by a Bee;
When they said, 'Does it buzz?' he replied, 'Yes it does!
It's a regular brute of a Bee!'

There was an Old Man with a flute,
A sarpint ran into his boot;
But he played day and night, till the sarpint took fright,
And avoided that man with a flute.

There was a Young Lady whose chin,
Resembled the point of a pin;
So she had it made sharp, and purchased a harp,
And played several tunes with her chin.

There was an Old Man in a boat,
Who said, 'I'm afloat! I'm afloat!'
When they said, 'No! you ain't!' he was ready to faint,
That unhappy Old Man in a boat.

There was a Young Lady of Portugal,
Whose ideas were excessively nautical;
She climbed up a tree, to examine the sea,
But declared she would never leave Portugal.

There was an Old Person of Leeds,
Whose head was infested with beads;
She sat on a stool, and ate gooseberry fool,
Which agreed with that person of Leeds.

There was a Young Person of Crete,
Whose toilette was far from complete;
She dressed in a sack, spickle-speckled with black,
That ombliferous person of Crete.

There was an Old Man who supposed,
That the street door was partially closed;
But some very large rats, ate his coats and his hats,
While that futile old gentleman dozed.

There was an Old Person whose habits,
Induced him to feed upon Rabbits;
When he'd eaten eighteen, he turned perfectly green,
Upon which he relinquished those habits.

There was an Old Person of Dover,
Who rushed through a field of blue Clover;
But some very large bees, stung his nose and his knees,
So he very soon went back to Dover.

There was an Old Person of Basing,
Whose presence of mind was amazing;
He purchased a steed, which he rode at full speed,
And escaped from the people of Basing.

There was an Old Person of Philæ,
Whose conduct was scroobious and wily;
He rushed up a Palm, when the weather was calm,
And observed all the ruins of Philæ.

There was an Old Man with a poker,
Who painted his face with red okre;
When they said, 'You're a Guy!' he made no reply,
But knocked them all down with his poker.

There was an Old Person of Mold,
Who shrank from sensations of cold;
So he purchased some muffs, some furs and some fluffs,
And wrapped himself from the cold.

There was an Old Man of Melrose,
Who walked on the tips of his toes;
But they said, 'It ain't pleasant, to see you at present,
You stupid Old Man of Melrose.'

There was a Young Lady of Lucca,
Whose lovers completely forsook her;
She ran up a tree, and said, 'Fiddle-de-dee!'
Which embarrassed the people of Lucca.

There was an Old Person of Cromer,
Who stood on one leg to read Homer;
When he found he grew stiff, he jumped over the cliff,
Which concluded that Person of Cromer.

There was an Old Person of Tring,
Who embellished his nose with a ring;
He gazed at the moon, every evening in June,
That ecstatic Old Person of Tring.

There was an Old Man on some rocks,
Who shut his wife up in a box;
When she said, 'Let me out,' he exclaimed, 'Without doubt,
You will pass all your life in that box.'

There was an Old Man in a pew,
Whose waistcoat was spotted with blue;
But he tore it in pieces, to give to his nieces, –
That cheerful Old Man in a pew.

There was an Old Man who said, 'How, –
Shall I flee from this horrible Cow?
I will sit on this stile, and continue to smile,
Which may soften the heart of that Cow.'

There was an Old Man of Whitehaven,
Who danced a quadrille with a Raven;
But they said – 'It's absurd, to encourage this bird!'
So they smashed that Old Man of Whitehaven.

There was an Old Person of Dutton,
Whose head was so small as a button;
So to make it look big, he purchased a wig,
And rapidly rushed about Dutton.

There was an Old Man who said, 'Hush!
I perceive a young bird in this bush!'
When they said – 'Is it small?' He replied – 'Not at all!
It is four times as big as the bush!'

There was an Old Person of Bangor,
Whose face was distorted with anger;
He tore off his boots, and subsisted on roots,
That borascible Person of Bangor.

There was an Old Man with a beard,
Who sat on a horse when he reared;
But they said, 'Never mind! you will fall off behind,
You propitious Old Man with a beard!'

There was an Old Person of Anerly,
Whose conduct was strange and unmannerly;
He rushed down the Strand, with a Pig in each hand,
But returned in the evening to Anerly.

There was an Old Person of Spain,
Who hated all trouble and pain;
So he sate on a chair, with his feet in the air,
That umbrageous Old Person of Spain.

There was an Old Man who said, 'Well!
Will *nobody* answer this bell?
I have pulled day and night, till my hair has grown white,
But nobody answers this bell!'

There was an Old Man with an owl,
Who continued to bother and howl;
He sate on a rail, and imbibed bitter ale,
Which refreshed that Old Man and his owl.

There was an Old Man at a casement,
Who held up his hands in amazement;
When they said, 'Sir! you'll fall!' he replied, 'Not at all!'
That incipient Old Man at a casement.

There was an Old Person of Ewell,
Who chiefly subsisted on gruel;
But to make it more nice, he inserted some mice,
Which refreshed that Old Person of Ewell.

There was an Old Man of Aôsta,
Who possessed a large Cow, but he lost her;
But they said, 'Don't you see, she has rushed up a tree?
You invidious Old Man of Aôsta!'

There was an Old Man, on whose nose,
Most birds of the air could repose;
But they all flew away, at the closing of day,
Which relieved that Old Man and his nose.

General appearance of a distinguished Landscapepainter – at Malta –
his hair having taken to a violent excess of growth of late.

Eggstracts from the Roehampton Chronicle

Object discovered in Lambda
16 August 1862

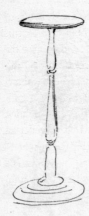

This remarkable instance of Snumphus, or Peppi-grottified Fungus, (growing on a lofty stalk or stem & resembling a Mushroom on Stilts,) has just been discovered in Lambda: – but at the time of our Reporter's departure, nothing was determined as to its previous=present, or past=future condition, nature, or circumstances. Our reeders shall however be jooly informed of any further inwestigations on the topic.

Object discovered in Lambda
September 28 1862

We are glad to present our readers with a concise and convalescent illustration of the most remarkable Object discovered in our age – & which is at present causing immense sensation & suffusion in the whole of the civilised world. – This, which is as interesting in its associations as it is singular & beautiful in form, is formed of a jetlike material with devellopements of gold borders all round it & the name 'Lambda' in distinct letters on its fuliginous face.

The use of the object is at present undetermined; – but it is obvious that it was once, (at an unbeknownly antique period,) the actual property of the illustrious & unfortunate Lambda.

That Lambda is not recorded by any authentic author to have been at Roehampton is advanced by some antiquarians who are desirous of diminishing the value of this priceless object as an objection to this theory: – but it does not follow that Lambda did not send or give the article in question to other persons. – And to all well conditioned individuals the simple fact of Lambda's name being written on the object itself is a full & painful guarantee of its indescribable interest.

Whether the Object in question be Lambda's Snuffbox, or Helmet, or Culinary=pipkin, – or dispatch box, time alone, that unveiler of obscure antidotes can eventually develllope: – but on those ignorant & disgusting creatures, who have ventured to suggest that this object is a Coalscuttle no further observation is necessary than that they cannot lay claim to the title of rational human beings, & that they ought to be altogether abolished & pisoned at the earliest aggravating & aggressive opportunity following this notice.

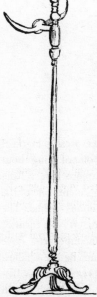

Object discovered in Thêta
November 1 1862

It is seldom that we have to call the attention of our readers to so many objects of antiquarian interest, discovered in one spot as the present latest & obviously melancholy article the portrait of which we subjoin, & which has been quite recently discovered in Thêta. Which its origin and use and effect are wholly, (if not almost,) unbeknown to the enlightened & choragic population of the surrounding hemisphere.

On the upper part of the perpendicular & columnar structure of the object is a cross bar – painfully suggestive of the manner in which the amiable Thêta met with her afflicting & philharmonic fate, – (such is the tradition of the country,) – by accidentally mistaking herself for a cloak & hanging herself on the obtrusive Cloak=peg till her futile & invaluable life was extinct. But there are others (it is due to the interests of science to state,) who contend that the singular object in question is the gigantic & fossil remnant of an extinct brute partaking of the nature of the ostrich & the domestic caterpillar, habitually walking on 3 feet, its neck, head, & expansive antennæ fixed on to the summit of its elongated body, & its general appearance at once surprising & objectionable. –

Of these conjectures, who shall say, which is the true, which the false, – or which the neither either one or t'other?

10   These doubts cannot be now obspiculated, nor indeed can they entirely be ever expressed. To give our readers an accurate portrait of the Object is our own sole & soporific duty.

Object discovered in Beta

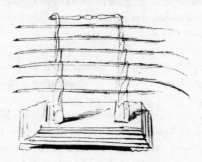

July 11 1863

We are delighted to acquaint our Readers, (& more especially Harkee! o logical Readers,) that fresh discoveries are on the point of being about to be expected to be supposed to be made at Clarence House Roehampton, – of which the accompanying drawing represents one of the most interesting hitherto offered to the pusillanimous public. The
20   object in question was found in Beta & is of an indescribable form & indefinable color: and although some idiotic contemporaries have argued that it is intended to hold pens, there cannot be the smallest doubt that it is the Stand on which the spears of the remarkable & distinguished Beta were kept when she was not using them. For it is well

known that Beta never grew to more than 3 feet 1 inch high – & consequently the penlike but warlike instruments above delineated are quite adapted to her size. Moreover their having been discovered in the apartment which for countless ages has been named after that small but indomitable person, is a parapumphilious proof that requires no other illustration except to the perception of owls, apes, geese, pigs, beetles, or donkies.

Q.E.D.

Letter to Ruth Decie

My dear little tiny child,

You will excuse my familiar mode of addressing you, because, you know, – you have as yet got no Christian name – ; – & to say – 'my dear Miss Decie' would be as much too formal, as 'my dear Decie' would be too rude. But as your Grandmama has written to me that you are just born I will write to congratulate you, & possibly this is one of the first letters you have as yet received. One of the old Greek Tragedians says – and I am sure you will not think me impertinent in translating what he says – μὴ φῦναι &c because there has not been time hitherto to buy you a Greek Dictionary, (& I feel sure you cannot read Sophocles without, – besides, the Dictionaries are so fat & heavy I am certain you could not use them comfortably to yourself & your nurse,) – μὴ φῦναι &c – which means 'it is better never to have [been] born at all, or if born, – to die as soon as possible.' But this I wholly dissent from: & on the contrary I congratulate you heartily on coming into a world where if we look for it there is far more good & pleasure than we can use up – even in the longest life. And you in particular will find that you have – all quite without any of your own exertions – a mother & a father, – a grandmother & a grandfather, – some uncles, – an extremely merry brother (who propels himself along the floor like a compasses,) a conservatory & a croquet ground, & a respectable old cove who is very fond of small children & will give you an Alphabet bye & bye. – I therefore advise you to live & laugh as long as you can for your own pleasure, & that of all your belongings.

Please tell your Grandmama that I also wished to stop when the carriage passed but couldn't – & say also, that I will write to her again shortly. And now my dear you have read enough for the present. Good night, & believe me,

> Your affte. old friend
> Edward Lear.

Give my love to your Papa & Mama.

There was an old person of Páxo,
Which complained when the fleas bit his back so;
  But they gave him a chair
  And impelled him to swear,
Which relieved that old person of Páxo.

'She sits upon her Bulbul'

She sits upon her Bulbul
  Through the long long hours of night –
And o'er the dark horizon gleams
  The Yashmack's fitful light.
The lone Yaourt sails slowly down
  The deep and craggy dell –
And from his lofty nest, loud screams
  The white-plumed Asphodel.

'O Digby my dear'

O Digby my dear
It is perfectly clear
   That my mind will be horridly vext,
If you happen to write,
By ill luck, to invite
   Me to dinner on Saturday next.

For this I should sigh at
That Mrs T Wyatt
   Already has booked me, o dear!
So I could not send answer
To you – 'I'm your man, Sir!' –
      Your loving fat friend,
        Edward Lear.

10

There was an old man with a Book –
Who said, 'Only look! Only look! –
   Obsquation, – obsgration, –
   At Waterloo station –
Enquire if there ain't such a Book!'

Letters to Evelyn Baring

Toosdy

Dear Baring, –

Disgustical to say, I must beg you to thank His Excellency from me, & to relate that I cannot come. I was engaged to dine with the De Vere's, but am too unwell with awful cold in the head & eyes to go out at all.

I have sent for 2 large tablecloths to blow my nose on, having already used up all my handkerchiefs. And altogether I am so unfit for company that I propose getting into a bag and being hung up to a bough of a tree till this tyranny is overpast. Please give the serming I send to His Excellency.

Yours sincerely,

Edward Lear

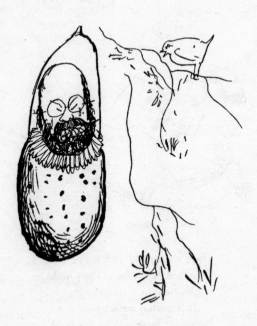

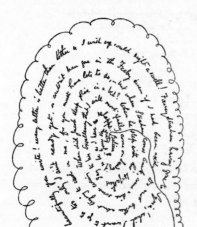

[my dear Baring how beautifully you write! every letter is better than t'other & I wish eye could right as well! Fancy Strahan having gone to Syria! which I want to go to too only I ain't ready yet, so couldn't have gone in the Feeby even if I had been ax'd. Do not bother about trying to cawl on me, for you must have lots to do, – but when Strahan comes back, come & dine some evening. When did Jacob sleep five in a bed? When he slep with his 4=fathers. Say to his Excellency that I will most gladly come on Sunday if so be as I have no relapps. Believe me, Yours sincerely]

10

[Feb. 19. 1864 Dear Baring Please give the encloged noat to Sir Henry – (which I had just written: – & say that I shall have great pleasure in coming on Sunday. I have sent your 2 vols of Hood to Wade Brown. Many thanks for lending them to me – which they have delighted me eggstreamly Yours sincerely]

[deerbaringiphowndacuppelloffotografsthismawningwitchisendjoo
thereiswunofeechsortsoyookankeepbothifyooliketodoosoanwenyoo=
=haveabetterwunofyourselfletmehavit.

Yossin seerly,
    DwdL[ear]]

Letter to Nora Decie

My dear Nora,

As it is most probable that you are less occupied than your mama or grandmama, I have written to you to beg you to tell them I am on the point of leaving Corfu, & that I am going to Athens & Candia, & may probably be in England by the end of June.

Will you say also that I am very sorry not to have been able to write all the winter, but I have done the same to everybody, & I don't think I shall ever write much more. I passed through Nice on my way hither but only arrived late at night & set off early next morning, but I wish
10 you could thank Mrs Riley for her letter – which was very useful. (*Nice* my dear does not mean *nice* (like sugarplums & pudding, –) but it is a town chockfull of houses, & it is called *Nice* as if it was written *niece*, which means Frank's daughter's relationship to you, only he has not got any daughters yet.)

Everybody here is packed up & going away, & we are all & every one of us cross & disagreeable & sorry & in a fuss & bothered. I should not however advise you to use the words 'bother' or 'chockfull' – for they are not strictly lady like expressions.

I hope Frank & Ruth are well, & your mother & father: give my love to them, & to your grandmama & grandpapa. Good bye my dear; I am going to start tomorrow, having sent my luggage away, & intending myself to go by sea, as it is cheaper than going by the steamer. I therefore join Captn. Deverill's 3 geese, & we are going to swim all the

way round Cape Matapan & so to the Piræus as fast as we can.

[Lear's adventures in Crete]

Plate 1

The Landscape painter perceives the Moufflons on the tops of the Mountains of Crete.

Plate 2

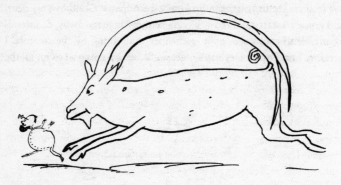

The Landscape painter escapes (with difficulty –) from an enraged Moufflon.

Plate 3

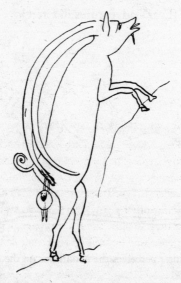

The landscape painter is enabled to ascend some of the highest tops of the Mountains of Crete by sticking on to a Moufflon's Horns.

Letters to Anna Duncan and Lady Duncan

Dear Miss Duncan,

[...] I got home very safely last night, and partly this was owing to the care taken of me by two remarkably large & amiable Frogs, whose arms I took, & who saw me down the lane. (You will see a true representation of the fact overleaf.) Nothing could exceed the genteel & intelligent expression of their countenances, except the urbanity of their deportment and the melancholy and oblivious sweetness of their voices. They informed me that they were the parents of nine and forty tadpoles of various ages and talents some of whom were expecting shortly to emigrate to Malvern and Mesopotamia.

Believe me,

    Yours sincerely,

      Edward Lear

My Dear Lady Duncan,

You & Miss Duncan will be much pleased to hear what occurred just after you left yesterday, & I am very sorry you had not happened to stay longer. Imagine how much surprised & gratified I was by a visit from the two considerate Frogs, who brought their two Eldest Tadpoles also to see me. On the other page you will see a correct drawing of the interview. Both of these amiable persons were much pleased with my 2 Lamps, which I regret I did not show you, & one of them was so good as to say that if he were able he would have tried to carry one of the Lamps as far as Maison Carab[ucel] to let you see it. They did not stay above 20 minutes, as they had a good way to go home, & I was vexed that there was nothing but a piece of cold lamb in the house & some

Marsala, both of which they declined, saying that either Watercresses or small beetles would have been pleasant, but that they were not hungry. I did not quite know at first how to be civil to the Tadpoles, as I found that owing to their long tails they could not sit on chairs as their parents did: I therefore put them into a wash-hand basin, & they seemed happy enough.

Such kind attentions from foreign persons quite of a different race, & I may say nature from our own, are certainly most delightful: and none the less so for being so unexpected. The Frogs were as good as to add that had I had any oil paintings they would have been glad to purchase one – but that the damp of their abode would quite efface watercolor art.

Believe me,

Yours sincerely,

Edward Lear

East of Frogs carrying Tadpoles

The History of the Seven Families of the Lake Pipple-Popple

CHAPTER I
INTRODUCTORY

In former days – that is to say, once upon a time, there lived in the Land of Grambleamble, Seven Families. They lived by the side of the great lake Pipple-Popple (one of the Seven Families, indeed, lived *in* the Lake), and on the outskirts of the City of Tosh, which, excepting when it was quite dark, they could see plainly. The names of all these places you have probably heard of, and you have only not to look in your Geography books to find out all about them.

Now the Seven Families who lived on the borders of the great lake   10
Pipple-Popple, were as follows in the next Chapter.

CHAPTER II
THE SEVEN FAMILIES

There was a Family of Two old Parrots and Seven young Parrots.

There was a Family of Two old Storks and Seven young Storks.

There was a Family of Two old Geese and Seven young Geese.

There was a Family of Two old Owls and Seven young Owls.

There was a Family of Two old Guinea Pigs and Seven young Guinea Pigs.

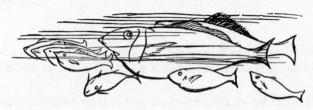

There was a Family of Two old Cats and Seven young Cats.

And there was a Family of Two old Fishes and Seven young Fishes.

CHAPTER III
THE HABITS OF THE
SEVEN FAMILIES

The Parrots lived upon the Soffsky-Poffsky trees, – which were beautiful to behold, and covered with blue leaves, – and they fed upon fruit, artichokes, and striped beetles.

The Storks walked in and out of the Lake Pipple-Popple, and ate frogs for breakfast and buttered toast for tea, but on account of the extreme length of their legs, they could not sit down, and so they walked about continually.

The Geese, having webs to their feet, caught quantities of flies, which they ate for dinner.

The Owls anxiously looked after mice, which they caught and made into sago puddings.

The Guinea Pigs toddled about the gardens, and ate lettuces and Cheshire cheese.

The Cats sate still in the sunshine, and fed upon sponge biscuits.

The Fishes lived in the Lake, and fed chiefly on boiled periwinkles.

And all these Seven Families lived together in the utmost fun and felicity.

CHAPTER IV
THE CHILDREN OF THE
SEVEN FAMILIES ARE SENT AWAY

One day all the Seven Fathers and the Seven Mothers of the Seven Families agreed that they would send their children out to see the world.

So they called them all together, and gave them each eight shillings and some good advice, some chocolate drops, and a small green morocco pocket-book to set down their expenses in.

They then particularly entreated them not to quarrel, and all the parents sent off their children with a parting injunction.

'If,' said the old Parrots, 'you find a Cherry, do not fight about who should have it.'

'And,' said the old Storks, 'if you find a Frog, divide it carefully into seven bits, but on no account quarrel about it.'

And the old Geese said to the Seven young Geese, 'Whatever you do, be sure you do not touch a Plum-pudding Flea.'

And the old Owls said, 'If you find a Mouse, tear him up into seven slices, and eat him cheerfully, but without quarrelling.'

And the old Guinea Pigs said, 'Have care that you eat your Lettuces, should you find any, not greedily but calmly.'

And the old Cats said, 'Be particularly careful not to meddle with a Clangle-Wangle, if you should see one.'

And the old Fishes said, 'Above all things avoid eating a blue Boss-woss, for they do not agree with Fishes, and give them a pain in their toes.'

So all the Children of each Family thanked their parents, and making in all forty-nine polite bows, they went into the wide world.

CHAPTER V
THE HISTORY OF THE
SEVEN YOUNG PARROTS

The Seven young Parrots had not gone far, when they saw a tree with a single Cherry on it, which the oldest Parrot picked instantly, but the other six, being extremely hungry, tried to get it also. On which all the Seven began to fight, and they scuffled,

and huffled,

and ruffled,

and shuffled,

and puffled,

and muffled,

and buffled,

and duffled,

and fluffled,

and guffled,

and bruffled, and

screamed, and shrieked, and squealed, and squeaked, and clawed, and snapped, and bit, and bumped, and thumped, and dumped, and flumped each other, till they were all torn into little bits, and at last

there was nothing left to record this painful incident, except the Cherry and seven small green feathers.

And that was the vicious and voluble end of the Seven young Parrots.

CHAPTER VI
THE HISTORY OF THE
SEVEN YOUNG STORKS

When the Seven young Storks set out, they walked or flew for fourteen weeks in a straight line, and for six weeks more in a crooked one; and after that they ran as hard as they could for one hundred and eight miles: and after that they stood still and made a himmeltanious chatter-clatter-blattery noise with their bills.

About the same time they perceived a large Frog, spotted with green, and with a sky-blue stripe under each ear.

So, being hungry, they immediately flew at him, and were going to divide him into seven pieces, when they began to quarrel as to which of his legs should be taken off first. One said this, and another said that, and while they were all quarrelling the Frog hopped away. And when they saw that he was gone, they began to chatter-clatter,

blatter-platter,

patter-blatter,

matter-clatter,

flatter-quatter,

more violently than ever. And after they had fought for a week they pecked each other all to little pieces, so that at last nothing was left of any of them except their bills.

And that was the end of the Seven young Storks.

CHAPTER VII
THE HISTORY OF THE
SEVEN YOUNG GEESE

When the Seven young Geese began to travel, they went over a large plain, on which there was but one tree, and that was a very bad one.

So four of them went up to the top of it, and looked about them, while the other three waddled up and down, and repeated poetry, and their last six lessons in Arithmetic, Geography, and Cookery.

Presently they perceived, a long way off, an object of the most interesting and obese appearance, having a perfectly round body, exactly resembling a boiled plum-pudding, with two little wings, and a beak, and three feathers growing out of his head, and only one leg.

So after a time all the Seven young Geese said to each other, 'Beyond all doubt this beast must be a Plum-pudding Flea!'

On which they incautiously began to sing aloud,

> 'Plum-pudding Flea,
> Plum-pudding Flea,
> Wherever you be,

O come to our tree,
And listen, O listen, O listen to me!'

And no sooner had they sung this verse than the Plum-pudding Flea began to hop and skip on his one leg with the most dreadful velocity, and came straight to the tree, where he stopped and looked about him in a vacant and voluminous manner.

On which the Seven young Geese were greatly alarmed, and all of a tremble-bemble; so one of them put out his long neck, and just touched him with the tip of his bill, – but no sooner had he done this than the Plum-pudding Flea skipped and hopped about more and more and higher and higher, after which he opened his mouth, and, to the great surprise and indignation of the Seven Geese, began to bark so loudly and furiously and terribly that they were totally unable to bear the noise, and by degrees every one of them suddenly tumbled down quite dead.

So that was the end of the Seven young Geese.

CHAPTER VIII
THE HISTORY OF THE
SEVEN YOUNG OWLS

When the Seven young Owls set out, they sate every now and then on the branches of the old trees, and never went far at one time.

And one night when it was quite dark, they thought they heard a Mouse, but as the gas lamps were not lighted, they could not see him.

So they called out, 'Is that a Mouse?'
On which a Mouse answered, 'Squeaky-peeky-weeky, yes it is.'
And immediately all the young Owls threw themselves off the tree,

meaning to alight on the ground; but they did not perceive that there
was a large well below them, into which they all fell superficially, and
were every one of them drowned in less than half a minute.

So that was the end of the Seven young Owls.

CHAPTER IX
THE HISTORY OF THE
SEVEN YOUNG GUINEA PIGS

10

The Seven young Guinea Pigs went into a garden full of Gooseberry-
bushes and Tiggory-trees, under one of which they fell asleep. When
they awoke, they saw a large Lettuce which had grown out of the
ground while they had been sleeping, and which had an immense num-
ber of green leaves. At which they all exclaimed,

> 'Lettuce! O Lettuce!
> Let us, O let us,
> O Lettuce leaves,
> O let us leave this tree and eat
> Lettuce, O let us, Lettuce leaves!'

20

And instantly the Seven young Guinea Pigs rushed with such
extreme force against the Lettuce-plant, and hit their heads so vividly

against its stalk, that the concussion brought on directly an incipient transitional inflammation of their noses, which grew worse and worse and worse and worse till it incidentally killed them all Seven.

And that was the end of the Seven young Guinea Pigs.

CHAPTER X
THE HISTORY OF THE
SEVEN YOUNG CATS

The Seven young Cats set off on their travels with great delight and rapacity. But, on coming to the top of a high hill, they perceived at a long distance off a Clangle-Wangle (or, as it is more properly written, Clangel-Wangel), and in spite of the warning they had had, they ran straight up to it.

(Now the Clangle-Wangle is a most dangerous and delusive beast, and by no means commonly to be met with. They live in the water as well as on land, using their long tail as a sail when in the former element. Their speed is extreme, but their habits of life are domestic and superfluous, and their general demeanour pensive and pellucid. On summer evenings they may sometimes be observed near the Lake Pipple-Popple, standing on their heads and humming their national melodies: they subsist entirely on vegetables, excepting when they eat veal, or mutton, or pork, or beef, or fish, or saltpetre.)

The moment the Clangle-Wangle saw the Seven young Cats approach, he ran away; and as he ran straight on for four months, and the Cats, though they continued to run, could never overtake him, – they all gradually *died* of fatigue and exhaustion, and never afterwards recovered.

And this was the end of the Seven young Cats.

CHAPTER XI
THE HISTORY OF THE
SEVEN YOUNG FISHES

The Seven young Fishes swam across the Lake Pipple-Popple, and into the river, and into the Ocean, where most unhappily for them, they saw on the 15th day of their travels, a bright blue Boss-Woss, and instantly swam after him. But the Boss-Woss plunged into a perpendicular,

       spicular,

        orbicular,

         quadrangular,

          circular depth of soft mud,

where in fact his house was.

10

And the Seven young Fishes, swimming with great and uncomfortable velocity, plunged also into the mud quite against their will, and not being accustomed to it, were all suffocated in a very short period.

And that was the end of the Seven young Fishes.

CHAPTER XII
OF WHAT OCCURRED SUBSEQUENTLY

After it was known that the Seven young Parrots,
            and the Seven young Storks,
            and the Seven young Geese,
            and the Seven young Owls,
            and the Seven young Guinea Pigs,
            and the Seven young Cats,
            and the Seven young Fishes,
10 were all dead, then the Frog, and the Plum-pudding Flea, and the
Mouse, and the Clangel-Wangel, and the Blue Boss-Woss,
all met together to rejoice over their good fortune.

   And they collected the Seven Feathers of the Seven young Parrots,
and the Seven Bills of the Seven young Storks, and the Lettuce, and the
Cherry, and having placed the latter on the Lettuce, and the other
objects in a circular arrangement at their base, they danced a hornpipe
round all these memorials until they were quite tired; after which they
gave a tea-party, and a garden-party, and a ball, and a concert, and then
returned to their respective homes full of joy and respect, sympathy,
20 satisfaction, and disgust.

CHAPTER XIII
OF WHAT BECAME OF THE PARENTS
OF THE FORTY-NINE CHILDREN

But when the two old Parrots,
      and the two old Storks,
      and the two old Geese,
      and the two old Owls,
      and the two old Guinea Pigs,
      and the two old Cats,
      and the two old Fishes,   10
became aware by reading in the newspapers, of the calamitous extinc-
tion of the whole of their families, they refused all further sustenance;
and sending out to various shops, they purchased great quantities of
Cayenne Pepper, and Brandy, and Vinegar, and blue Sealing-wax,
besides Seven immense glass Bottles with air-tight stoppers. And hav-
ing done this, they ate a light supper of brown bread and Jerusalem
Artichokes, and took an affecting and formal leave of the whole of their
acquaintance, which was very numerous and distinguished, and select,
and responsible, and ridiculous.

CHAPTER XIV   20
CONCLUSION

And after this, they filled the bottles with the ingredients for pickling,
and each couple jumped into a separate bottle, by which effort of
course they all died immediately, and became thoroughly pickled in a
few minutes; having previously made their wills (by the assistance of
the most eminent Lawyers of the District), in which they left strict
orders that the Stoppers of the Seven Bottles should be carefully sealed
up with the blue Sealing-wax they had purchased; and that they them-
selves in the Bottles should be presented to the principal museum of the
city of Tosh, to be labelled with Parchment or any other anti-congenial   30
succedaneum, and to be placed on a marble table with silver-gilt legs,

for the daily inspection and contemplation, and for the perpetual benefit of the pusillanimous public.

And if ever you happen to go to Gramble-Blamble, and visit that museum in the city of Tosh, look for them on the Ninety-eighth table in the Four hundred and twenty-seventh room of the right-hand corridor of the left wing of the Central Quadrangle of that magnificent building; for if you do not, you certainly will not see them.

The Duck and the Kangaroo

Said the Duck to the Kangaroo,
  'Good gracious! how you hop!
Over the fields and the water too,
  As if you never would stop!
My life is a bore in this nasty pond,
And I long to go out in the world beyond!
  I wish I could hop like you!'
  Said the Duck to the Kangaroo.

'Please give me a ride on your back!'
  Said the Duck to the Kangaroo.   10
'I would sit quite still, and say nothing but "Quack,"
  The whole of the long day through!
And we'd go to the Dee, and the Jelly Bo Lee,
Over the land, and over the sea; –
  Please take me a ride! O do!'
  Said the Duck to the Kangaroo.

Said the Kangaroo to the Duck,
   'This requires some little reflection;
Perhaps on the whole it might bring me luck,
   And there seems but one objection,
Which is, if you'll let me speak so bold,
Your feet are unpleasantly wet and cold,
   And would probably give me the roo-
   matiz!' said the Kangaroo.

Said the Duck, 'As I sate on the rocks,
   I have thought over that completely,
And I bought four pairs of worsted socks
   Which fit my web-feet neatly.
And to keep out the cold I've bought a cloak,
And every day a cigar I'll smoke,
   All to follow my own dear true
   Love of a Kangaroo!'

Said the Kangaroo, 'I'm ready!
   All in the moonlight pale;
But to balance me well, dear Duck, sit steady!
   And quite at the end of my tail!'
So away they went with a hop and a bound,
And they hopped the whole world three times round;
   And who so happy, – O who,
     As the Duck and the Kangaroo?

    40

'Gozo my child is the isle of Calypso'

Gozo my child is the isle of Calypso
That naughty young woman who made egg flip so
And all day long with a spoon did sip so,
And every morn in the sea did dip so
Whereon Ulysses seeing her strip so
And all her beautiful ringlets drip so
From her beautiful head to her beautiful hipso
Because her curls she never would clip so,
– Took to staying away from his ship so,
And she his mariners all did tip so
And fed them with chickens that had the pip so
For fear he should ever give her the slip so
And over the ocean start for a trip so
    Singing – (with peculiar sweetness–) 'This is
I who have wheedled the wily Ulysses,
With kurls and kobwebs and kustards and kisses
    Gip so, whip so, crip so, and quip so
    Flip so, bip so, rip so and zip so –
      O naughty Calypso!
    Which made the little hills for to skip so!'

Stratford Place Gazette

7th August 1866
(9534th Edition)

ALARMING AND HORRIBLE EVENT

We regret to state that at 4 P.M. this day the well known Author &
Landscape painter Edward Lear committed sukycide by throwing
hisself out of a 5 pair of stairs winder. The cause of this amazing &
obsequious conclusion to a well spent & voracious life, we understand
to be as follies: – Mr L, having returned from a visit to some friends at
Hastings, wrote to them on his return to London begging them immee-   10
jiately to forward a book called 'The Gothe & the Un' which he
supposed he had left at their house. On this day however, the said book
tumbled spongetaneously out of a coat which had not been opened or
shaken or examined or craxpaxified in any way whatsoever; on seeing
which the unfortunate Gentleman tore his hair promiscuous, & bitter-
ly reproached his self with the trouble he had given to Mrs and Mr G.

Scrivens, likewise Mr Bennell: & finally giving way to dishpear, opened the window & leaped 4th into the street – to the extreme surprise & delight of some little children playing on the pavement, – the alarm of the thinking part of the neighbourhood, & the eminent annoyance to his own ribs and existence. Our readers will doubtless drop a tear over this brutal & harmonious occurrence, a view of which, (sketched by our special artist who happened to be passing,) we present them with our liveliest regards & compliments.

[Three miscellaneous limericks]

There was an old person who said –
'Do you think I've a very large head?'

There was an old man who felt pert
When he wore a pale rosecoloured shirt.
　　When they said – 'Is it pleasant?'
　　He cried – 'Not at present –
It's a *leetle* too short – is my shirt!'

There was an old person who sung,
'Bloo – Sausages! Kidnies! and Tongue!
　　Bloo! Bloo! my dear Madam,
　　My name is Old Adam.
Bloo! Sausages – Kidnies, and Tongue!'

The Adventures of Mr Lear & the Polly [& the] Pusseybite on their way to the Ritertitle Mountains

Mr Lear goes out a walking with a Polly & the Pusseybite.

Mr Lear, feeling tired, & also the Polly & the Pusseybite, sit down on a wall to rest.

Mr Lear, the Polly & the Pusseybite go into a shop to buy a Numbrella, because it began to rain.

Mr L., the P. & the P.B. having purchased umbrellas, proceed on their walk.

Mr L. & the P. & the P.B. arrive at a bridge, which being broken they do not know what to do.

Mr L., the P. & the P.B. all tumble promiscuous into the raging river & become quite wet.

[lacuna]

Mr Lear & the P. & the P.B. pursue their journey in a benevolent boat.

Mr L. & the P. & the P.B. incidentally fall over an unexpected Cataract, & are all dashed [to] atoms.

[lacuna]

The 2 venerable Jebusites fasten the remains of Mr L., the P. & the P.B.
together, but fail to reconstruct them perfectly as 3 individuals.

Mr Lear & the Pusseybite & the Polly cat & the 2 Jebusites & the
Jerusalem Artichokes and the Octagonal Oysterclippers all tumble into
a deep hole & are never seen or distinguished or heard of never more
afterwards.

'O Thuthan Thmith! Thweet Thuthan Thmith!'

My dear Mitheth Digby,
Thankth for your note: I will come on Thunday. But whatth been a
matter with Digby? I hope he ith better than he wath. I am compoth-
ing a thong to thing now that my teeth have thuffered tho mutth, & it
theemth to me that it will produthe a thenthation in the muthical
thphereth.

> O Thuthan Thmith! Thweet Thuthan Thmith!
> I thit in thilenth clothe to thee
> And lithtning to thy thongthtreth lipth
> I watth the tholemn thtately thipth
> Acroth the thounding thilver thea!
> >   And thith – o! thith!
> >   I thay ith blith –
> >   Thweet Thuthan Thmith!
> >   Thweet Thuthan Thmith!

> The thlender Thrimp itth gambolth playth,
> The thiny thprightly fitheth thwim, –
> The thandy thore, the dithtant hillth, –
> All thethe I watth; – but nothing thillth
> The thindy that my bothom fillth
> In gathing on thy thape tho thlim!
> >   With burthting thobth
> >   My thoft thoul throbth –
> >   Thweet Thuthan Thmith!
> >   Thweet Thuthan Thmith!

10

I hope, if I publith thith that you will thubthcribe for thikthty or
theventy copieth.
> My love to Digby.
> >   Yourth thintherely,
> >   > Edw Lear.

The Story of the Four Little Children Who Went Round the World

Once upon a time, a long while ago, there were four little people whose names were

VIOLET,   SLINGSBY,   GUY, and LIONEL;

and they all thought they should like to see the world. So they bought a large boat to sail quite round the world by sea, and then they were to come back on the other side by land. The boat was painted blue with green spots, and the sail was yellow with red stripes; and when they set off, they only took a small Cat to steer and look after the boat, besides an elderly Quangle-Wangle, who had to cook the dinner and make the
10 tea; for which purposes they took a large kettle.

For the first ten days they sailed on beautifully, and found plenty to eat, as there were lots of fish, and they had only to take them out of the sea with a long spoon, when the Quangle-Wangle instantly cooked them, and the Pussy-cat was fed with the bones, with which she expressed herself pleased on the whole, so that all the party were very happy.

During the day-time, Violet chiefly occupied herself in putting salt-water into a churn, while her three brothers churned it violently, in the hope that it would turn into butter, which it seldom, if ever did; and in the evening they all retired into the Tea-kettle, where they all managed to sleep very comfortably, while Pussy and the Quangle-Wangle managed the boat.

After a time they saw some land at a distance; and when they came to it, they found it was an island made of water quite surrounded by earth. Besides that, it was bordered by evanescent isthmusses with a great Gulf-stream running about all over it, so that it was perfectly beautiful, and contained only a single tree, 503 feet high.

When they had landed, they walked about, but found to their great surprise, that the island was quite full of veal-cutlets and chocolate-drops, and nothing else. So they all climbed up the single high tree to discover, if possible, if there were any people; but having remained on the top of the tree for a week, and not seeing anybody, they naturally concluded that there were no inhabitants, and accordingly when they came down, they loaded the boat with two thousand veal-cutlets and a million of chocolate drops, and these afforded them sustenance for more than a month, during which time they pursued their voyage with the utmost delight and apathy.

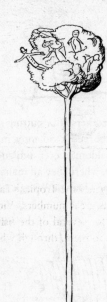

After this they came to a shore where there were no less than sixty-five great red parrots with blue tails, sitting on a rail all of a row, and all fast asleep. And I am sorry to say that the Pussy-cat and the Quangle-Wangle crept softly and bit off the tail-feathers of all the sixty-five parrots, for which Violet reproved them both severely.

Notwithstanding which, she proceeded to insert all the feathers, two hundred and sixty in number, in her bonnet, thereby causing it to have a lovely and glittering appearance, highly prepossessing and efficacious.

The next thing that happened to them was in a narrow part of the sea, which was so entirely full of fishes that the boat could go on no further; so they remained there about six weeks, till they had eaten nearly all the fishes, which were Soles, and all ready-cooked and covered with shrimp sauce, so that there was no trouble whatever. And as the few fishes who remained uneaten complained of the cold, as well as of the difficulty they had in getting any sleep on account

10

of the extreme noise made by the Arctic Bears and the Tropical Turn-spits which frequented the neighbourhood in great numbers, Violet most amiably knitted a small woollen frock for several of the fishes, and Slingsby administered some opium drops to them, through which kindness they became quite warm and slept soundly.

20

Then they came to a country which was wholly covered with immense Orange-trees of a vast size, and quite full of fruit. So they all landed, taking with them the Tea-kettle, intending to gather some of the Oranges and place them in it. But while they were busy about this, a most dreadfully high wind rose, and blew out most of the Parrot-tail feathers from Violet's bonnet. That, however, was nothing compared with the calamity of the Oranges falling down on their heads by millions and millions, which thumped and bumped and bumped and thumped them all so seriously that they were obliged to run as hard as they could for their lives, besides that the sound of the Oranges rattling on the Tea-kettle was of the most fearful and amazing nature.

Nevertheless they got safely to the boat, although considerably vexed and hurt; and the Quangle-Wangle's right foot was so knocked about, that he had to sit with his head in his slipper for at least a week.

This event made them all for a time rather melancholy, and perhaps they might never have become less so, had not Lionel with a most praiseworthy devotion and perseverance, continued to stand on one leg and whistle to them in a loud and lively manner, which diverted the whole party so extremely, that they gradually recovered their spirits, and agreed that whenever they should reach home they would subscribe towards a testimonial to Lionel, entirely made of Ginger-bread and Raspberries, as an earnest token of their sincere and grate-ful infection.

After sailing on calmly for several more days, they came to another country, where they were much pleased and surprised to see a countless

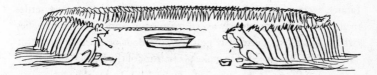

multitude of white Mice with red eyes, all sitting in a great circle, slow-ly eating Custard Pudding with the most satisfactory and polite demeanour.

And as the Four Travellers were rather hungry, being tired of eating nothing but Soles and Oranges for so long a period, they held a coun-cil as to the propriety of asking the Mice for some of their Pudding in a humble and affecting manner, by which they could hardly be other-wise than gratified. It was agreed therefore that Guy should go and ask the Mice, which he immediately did; and the result was that they gave [him] a Walnut-shell only half full of Custard diluted with water. Now, this displeased Guy, who said, 'Out of such a lot of Pudding as you have got, I must say you might have spared a somewhat larger quantity!' But no sooner had he finished speaking than all the Mice turned round at once, and sneezed at him in an appalling and vindictive manner, (and it

is impossible to imagine a more scroobious and unpleasant sound than that caused by the simultaneous sneezing of many millions of angry Mice,) so that Guy rushed back to the boat, having first shied his cap into the middle of the Custard Pudding, by which means he complete-ly spoiled the Mice's dinner.

By-and-by the Four Children came to a country where there were no houses, but only an incredibly innumerable number of large bottles without corks, and of a dazzling and sweetly susceptible blue colour. Each of these blue bottles contained a Blue-Bottle-Fly, and all these interesting animals live continually together in the most copious and rural harmony, nor perhaps in many parts of the world is such perfect and abject happiness to be found. Violet, and Slingsby, and Guy, and Lionel, were greatly struck with this singular and instructive settlement, and having previously asked permission of the Blue-Bottle-Flies
10 (which was most courteously granted), the Boat was drawn up to the shore and they proceeded to make tea in front of the Bottles; but as they

had no tea-leaves, they merely placed some pebbles in the hot water, and the Quangle-Wangle played some tunes over it on an Accordion, by which of course tea was made directly, and of the very best quality.

The Four Children then entered into conversation with the Blue-Bottle-Flies, who discoursed in a placid and genteel manner, though with a slightly buzzing accent, chiefly owing to the fact that they each held a small clothes-brush between their teeth which naturally occasioned a fizzy extraneous utterance.

20 'Why,' said Violet, 'would you kindly inform us, do you reside in bottles? and if in bottles at all, why not rather in green or purple, or indeed in yellow bottles?'

To which questions a very aged Blue-Bottle-Fly answered, 'We found the bottles here all ready to live in, that is to say, our great-great-great-great-great-grandfathers did, so we occupied them at once. And when the winter comes on, we turn the bottles upside-down, and consequently rarely feel the cold at all, and you know very well that this could not be the case with bottles of any other colour than blue.'

'Of course it could not,' said Slingsby, 'but if we may take the liber-
30 ty of inquiring, on what do you chiefly subsist?'

'Mainly on Oyster-patties,' said the Blue-Bottle-Fly, 'and, when these are scarce, on Raspberry Vinegar and Russian leather boiled down to a jelly.'

'How delicious!' said Guy.

To which Lionel added, 'Huzz!' and all the Blue-Bottle-Flies said 'Buzz!'

At this time, an elderly Fly said it was the hour for the Evening-song to be sung; and on a signal being given all the Blue-Bottle-Flies began to buzz at once in a sumptuous and sonorous manner, the melodious and mucilaginous sounds echoing all over the waters, and resounding across the tumultuous tops of the transitory Titmice upon the intervening and verdant mountains, with a serene and sickly suavity only known to the truly virtuous. The Moon was shining slobaciously from the star-bespringled sky, while her light irrigated the smooth and shiny sides and wings and backs of the Blue-Bottle-Flies with a peculiar and trivial splendour, while all nature cheerfully responded to the cerul and conspicuous circumstances.

In many long-after years, the Four little Travellers looked back that evening as one of the happiest in all their lives, and it was already past midnight, when – the Sail of the Boat having been set up by the Quangle-Wangle, the Tea-kettle and Churn placed in their respective positions, and the Pussy-cat stationed at the Helm – the Children took a last and affectionate farewell of the Blue-Bottle-Flies, who walked down in a body to the water's edge to see the Travellers embark.

As a token of parting respect and esteem, Violet made a curtsey quite down to the ground, and stuck one of her few remaining Parrot

feathers into the back hair of the most pleasing of the Blue-Bottle-Flies, while Slingsby, Guy, and Lionel offered them three small boxes, containing respectively, Black Pins, Dried Figs, and Epsom Salts: and thus they left that happy shore for ever.

Overcome by their feelings, the Four little Travellers instantly jumped into the Tea-kettle, and fell fast asleep. But all along the shore for many hours there was distinctly heard a sound of severely suppressed sobs, and of a vague multitude of living creatures using their pocket-handkerchiefs in a subdued simultaneous snuffle – lingering sadly along the wallopping waves as the boat sailed farther and farther away from the Land of the Happy Blue-Bottle-Flies.

Nothing particular occurred for some days after these events, except that as the Travellers were passing a low tract of sand, they perceived an unusual and gratifying spectacle, namely, a large number of Crabs and Crawfish – perhaps six or seven hundred – sitting by the water-side, and endeavouring to disentangle a vast heap of pale pink worsted, which they moistened at intervals with a fluid composed of Lavender-water and White-wine Negus.

'Can we be of any service to you, O crusty Crabbies?' said the Four Children.

'Thank you kindly,' said the Crabs, consecutively. 'We are trying to make some worsted Mittens, but do not know how.'

On which Violet, who was perfectly acquainted with the art of mitten-making, said to the Crabs, 'Do your claws unscrew, or are they fixtures?'

'They are all made to unscrew,' said the Crabs, and forthwith they deposited a great pile of claws close to the boat, with which Violet uncombed all the pale pink worsted, and then made the loveliest Mittens with it you can imagine. These the Crabs, having resumed and screwed on their claws, placed cheerfully upon their wrists, and walked away rapidly on their hind-legs, warbling songs with a silvery voice and in a minor key.

After this the Four little People sailed on again till they came to a vast and wide plain of astonishing dimensions, on which nothing whatever could be discovered at first; but as the Travellers walked onward, there appeared in the extreme and dim distance a single object, which on a nearer approach and on an accurately cutaneous inspection, seemed to be somebody in a large white wig sitting on an arm-chair made of Sponge Cakes and Oyster-shells. 'It does not quite look like a human being,' said Violet, doubtfully; nor could they make out what it

really was, till the Quangle-Wangle (who had previously been round
the world), exclaimed softly in a loud voice, 'It is the Co-operative
Cauliflower!'

And so in truth it was, and they soon found that what they had taken
for an immense wig was in reality the top of the cauliflower, and that
he had no feet at all, being able to walk tolerably well with a fluctuat-
ing and graceful movement on a single cabbage stalk, an accomplish-
ment which naturally saved him the expense of stockings and shoes.

Presently, while the whole party from the boat was gazing at him
with mingled affection and disgust, he suddenly arose, and in a some-   10
what plumdomphious manner hurried off towards the setting sun, – his
legs supported by two superincumbent confidential cucumbers, and a
large number of Waterwagtails proceeding in advance of him by three-

and-three in a row – till he finally disappeared on the brink of the west-
ern sky in a crystal cloud of sudorific sand.

So remarkable a sight of course impressed the Four Children very
deeply; and they returned immediately to their boat with a strong sense
of undeveloped asthma and a great appetite.

Shortly after this the Travellers were obliged to sail directly below
some high overhanging rocks, from the top of one of which, a particu-   20
larly odious little boy, dressed in rose-coloured knickerbockers, and
with a pewter plate upon his head, threw an enormous Pumpkin at the
boat, by which it was instantly upset.

But this upsetting was of no consequence, because all the party knew how to swim very well, and in fact they preferred swimming about till after the moon rose, when the water growing chilly, they sponge-taneously entered the boat. Meanwhile the Quangle-Wangle threw back the Pumpkin with immense force, so that it hit the rocks where the malicious little boy in rose-coloured knickerbockers was sitting, when, being quite full of Lucifer-matches, the Pumpkin exploded sur-reptitiously into a thousand bits, whereon the rocks instantly took fire, and the odious little boy became unpleasantly hotter and hotter and hotter, till his knickerbockers were turned quite green, and his nose was burned off.

Two or three days after this had happened, they came to another place, where they found nothing at all except some wide and deep pits full of Mulberry Jam. This is the property of the tiny Yellow-nosed Apes who abound in these districts, and who store up the Mulberry Jam for their food in winter, when they mix it with pellucid pale peri-winkle soup, and serve it out in Wedgwood China bowls, which grow freely all over that part of the country. Only one of the Yellow-nosed Apes was on the spot, and he was fast asleep: yet the Four Travellers and the Quangle-Wangle and Pussy were so terrified by the violence and sanguinary sound of his snoring, that they merely took a small cup-ful of the Jam, and returned to re-embark in their Boat without delay.

What was their horror on seeing the boat (including the Churn and the Tea-kettle), in the mouth of an enormous Seeze Pyder, an aquatic and ferocious creature truly dreadful to behold, and happily only met with in these excessive longitudes. In a moment the beautiful boat was bitten into fifty-five-thousand-million-hundred-billion bits; and it instantly became quite clear that Violet, Slingsby, Guy, and Lionel could no longer preliminate their voyage by sea.

The Four Travellers were therefore obliged to resolve on pursuing their wanderings by land, and very fortunately there happened to pass by at that moment, an elderly Rhinoceros, on which they seized; and all four mounting on his back, the Quangle-Wangle sitting on his horn

and holding on by his ears, the Pussy-cat swinging at the end of his tail, they set off, having only four small beans and three pounds of mashed potatoes to last through their whole journey.

They were, however, able to catch numbers of the chickens and turkeys, and other birds who incessantly alighted on the head of the Rhinoceros for the purpose of gathering the seeds of the rhododendron plants which grew there, and these creatures they cooked in the most translucent and satisfactory manner, by means of a fire lighted on the end of the Rhinoceros' back. A crowd of Kangaroos and Gigantic Cranes accompanied them, from feelings of curiosity and complacency, so that they were never at a loss for company, and went onward as it were in a sort of profuse and triumphant procession.

Thus, in less than eighteen weeks, they all arrived safely at home, where they were received by their admiring relatives with joy tempered with contempt; and where they finally resolved to carry out the rest of their travelling plans at some more favourable opportunity.

As for the Rhinoceros, in token of their grateful adherence, they had him killed and stuffed directly, and then set him up outside the door of their father's house as a Diaphanous Doorscraper.

Growling Eclogue
Composed at Cannes, December 9th, 1867

(Interlocutors – Mr Lear and Mr and Mrs Symonds)

Edwardus. – What makes you look so black, so glum, so cross?
　　　　　　Is it neuralgia, headache, or remorse?

Johannes. – What makes you look as cross, or even more so?
　　　　　　Less like a man than is a broken Torso?

　　E. – What if my life is odious, should I grin?
　　　　　If you are savage, need I care a pin?

　　J. – And if I suffer, am I then an owl?
　　　　　May I not frown and grind my teeth and growl?

　　E. – Of course you may; but may not I growl too?
　　　　　May I not frown and grind my teeth like you?　　　　10

　　J. – See Catherine comes! To her, to her,
　　　　　Let each his several miseries refer;
　　　　　She shall decide whose woes are least or worst,
　　　　　And which, as growler, shall rank last or first.

Catherine. – Proceed to growl, in silence I'll attend,
　　　　　　And hear your foolish growlings to the end;
　　　　　　And when they're done, I shall correctly judge
　　　　　　Which of your griefs are real or only fudge.
　　　　　　Begin, let each his mournful voice prepare,
　　　　　　(And, pray, however angry, do not swear!)　　　　20

　　J. – We came abroad for warmth, and find sharp cold!
　　　　　Cannes is an imposition, and we're sold.

　　E. – Why did I leave my native land, to find
　　　　　Sharp hailstones, snow, and most disgusting wind?

J. –   What boots it that we orange trees or lemons see,
       If we must suffer from *such* vile inclemency?

E. –   Why did I take the lodgings I have got,
       Where all I don't want is: – all I want not?

J. –   Last week I called aloud, O! O! O! O!
       The ground is wholly overspread with snow!
       Is that at any rate a theme for mirth
       Which makes a sugar-cake of all the earth?

E. –   Why must I sneeze and snuffle, groan and cough,
       If my hat's on my head, or if it's off?
       Why must I sink all poetry in this prose,
       The everlasting blowing of my nose?

J. –   When I walk out the mud my footsteps clogs,
       Besides, I suffer from attacks of dogs.

E. –   Me a vast awful bulldog, black and brown,
       Completely terrified when near the town;
       As calves, perceiving butchers, trembling reel,
       So did *my* calves the approaching monster feel.

J. –   Already from two rooms we're driven away,
       Because the beastly chimneys smoke all day:
       Is this a trifle, say? Is this a joke?
       That we, like hams, should be becooked in smoke?

E. –   Say! what avails it that my servant speaks
       Italian, English, Arabic, and Greek,
       Besides Albanian: if he don't speak French,
       How can he ask for salt, or shrimps, or tench?

J. –   When on the foolish hearth fresh wood I place,
       It whistles, sings, and squeaks, before my face:
       And if it does unless the fire burns bright,
       And if it does, yet squeaks, how can I write?

E. – Alas! I needs must go and call on swells,
That they may say, 'Pray draw me the Estrelles.'
On one I went last week to leave a card,
The swell was out – the servant eyed me hard:
'This chap's a thief disguised,' his face expressed:
If I go there again, may I be blest!   60

J. – Why must I suffer in this wind and gloom?
Roomattics in a vile cold attic room?

E. – Swells drive about the road with haste and fury,
As Jehu drove about all over Jewry.
Just now, while walking slowly, I was all but
Run over by the Lady Emma Talbot,
Whom not long since a lovely babe I knew,
With eyes and cap-ribbons of perfect blue.

J. – Downstairs and upstairs, every blessed minute,
There's each room with pianofortes in it.   70
How can I write with noises such as those?
And, being always discomposed, compose?

E. – Seven Germans through my garden lately strayed,
And all on instruments of torture played;
They blew, they screamed, they yelled: how can I paint
Unless my room is quiet, which it ain't?

J. – How can I study if a hundred flies
Each moment blunder into both my eyes?

E. – How can I draw with green or blue or red,
If flies and beetles vex my old bald head?   80

J. – How can I translate German Metaphys-
ics, if mosquitoes round my forehead whizz?

E. – I've bought some bacon, (though it's much too fat,)
But round the house there prowls a hideous cat:

Once should I see my bacon in her mouth,
What care I if my rooms look north or south?

J. – Pain from a pane in one cracked window comes,
Which sings and whistles, buzzes, shrieks and hums;
In vain amain with pain the pane with this chord
90   I fain would strain to stop the beastly *dis*cord!

E. – If rain and wind and snow and such like ills
Continue here, how shall I pay my bills?
For who through cold and slush and rain will come
To see my drawings and to purchase some?
And if they don't, what destiny is mine?
How can I ever get to Palestine?

J. – The blinding sun strikes through the olive trees,
When I walk out, and always makes me sneeze.

E. – Next door, if all night long the moon is shining,
100   There sits a dog, who wakes me up with whining.

Cath. – Forbear! You both are bores, you've growled enough:
No longer will I listen to such stuff!
All men have nuisances and bores to afflict 'um:
Hark then, and bow to my official dictum!

For you, Johannes, there is most excuse,
(Some interruptions are the very deuce,)
You're younger than the other cove, who surely
Might have some sense – besides, you're somewhat
    poorly.
This therefore is my sentence, that you nurse
110   The Baby for seven hours, and nothing worse.
For you, Edwardus, I shall say no more
Than that your griefs are fudge, yourself a bore:
Return at once to cold, stewed, minced, hashed
    mutton –
To wristbands ever guiltless of a button –

To raging winds and sea, (where don't you wish
Your luck may ever let you catch one fish?) –
To make large drawings nobody will buy –
To paint oil pictures which will never dry –
To write new books which nobody will read –
To drink weak tea, on tough old pigs to feed –   120
Till spring-time brings the birds and leaves and flowers,
And time restores a world of happier hours.

The Owl and the Pussy-cat

The Owl and the Pussy-cat went to sea
      In a beautiful pea-green boat,
They took some honey, and plenty of money,
      Wrapped up in a five-pound note.
The Owl looked up to the stars above,
      And sang to a small guitar,
'O lovely Pussy! O Pussy, my love,
      What a beautiful Pussy you are,
            You are,
            You are!
What a beautiful Pussy you are!'

Pussy said to the Owl, 'You elegant fowl!
      How charmingly sweet you sing!
O let us be married! too long we have tarried:
      But what shall we do for a ring?'
They sailed away, for a year and a day,
      To the land where the Bong-tree grows,
And there in a wood a Piggy-wig stood,
      With a ring at the end of his nose,
            His nose,
            His nose,
With a ring at the end of his nose.

'Dear Pig, are you willing to sell for one shilling
    Your ring?' Said the Piggy, 'I will.'
So they took it away, and were married next day
    By the Turkey who lives on the hill.
They dinèd on mince, and slices of quince,
    Which they ate with a runcible spoon;
And hand in hand, on the edge of the sand,
    They danced by the light of the moon,   30
        The moon,
        The moon,
They danced by the light of the moon.

[Mrs Blue Dickey-bird]

Mrs Blue Dickey-bird, who went out a-walking with her six chickey
   birds: she carried a parasol and wore a bonnet of green silk.
The first little chickey bird had daisies growing out of his head, and
   wore boots because of the dirt.
The second little chickey bird wore a hat, for fear it should rain.
The third little chickey bird carried a jug of water.
The fourth little chickey bird carried a muff, to keep her wings warm.
The fifth little chickey bird was round as a ball.
And the sixth little chickey bird walked on his head, to save his feet.

'Some people their attention fixes'

Some people their attention fixes
On 'Istory or Polly=tixes
Some studies French, & some Hastronomy
And others cultivates Heconomy.

The Broom, the Shovel, the Poker, and the Tongs

The Broom and the Shovel, the Poker and Tongs,
    They all took a drive in the Park,
And they each sang a song, Ding-a-dong, Ding-a-dong,
    Before they went back in the dark.
Mr Poker he sate quite upright in the coach,
    Mr Tongs made a clatter and clash,
Miss Shovel was dressed all in black (with a brooch),
    Mrs Broom was in blue (with a sash).
        Ding-a-dong! Ding-a-dong!
        And they all sang a song!   10

'Oh Shovely so lovely!' the Poker he sang,
    'You have perfectly conquered my heart!
Ding-a-dong! Ding-a-dong! If you're pleased with my song,
    I will feed you with cold apple tart!
When you scrape up the coals with a delicate sound,
    You enrapture my life with delight!
Your nose is so shiny! your head is so round!
    And your shape is so slender and bright!
        Ding-a-dong! Ding-a-dong!
        Ain't you pleased with my song?'   20

'Alas! Mrs Broom !' sighed the Tongs in his song,
　　'O is it because I'm so thin,
And my legs are so long – Ding-a-dong! Ding-a-dong!
　　That you don't care about me a pin?
Ah! fairest of creatures, when sweeping the room,
　　Ah! why don't you heed my complaint!
Must you needs be so cruel, you beautiful Broom,
　　Because you are covered with paint?
　　　　Ding-a-dong! Ding-a-dong!
30　　　You are certainly wrong!'

Mrs Broom and Miss Shovel together they sang,
　　'What nonsense you're singing to-day!'
Said the Shovel, 'I'll certainly hit you a bang!'
　　Said the Broom, 'And I'll sweep you away!'
So the Coachman drove homeward as fast as he could,
　　Perceiving their anger with pain;
But they put on the kettle, and little by little,
　　They all became happy again.
　　　　Ding-a-dong! Ding-a-dong!
40　　　There's an end of my song!

There was an old man who said – 'Hum!
I am always a-spraining my Thumb.'
    When they said 'Tell us how?'
    He made them a bow, –
And said, 'I've no jints in my Thumb!'

Calico Pie

Calico Pie,
The little birds fly
Down to the calico tree,
  Their wings were blue,
  And they sang 'Tilly-loo!'
  Till away they flew, –
And they never came back to me!
  They never came back!
  They never came back!
They never came back to me!

Calico Jam,
The little Fish swam,
Over the syllabub sea,
  He took off his hat,
  To the Sole and the Sprat,
  And the Willeby-wat, –

But he never came back to me!
  He never came back!
  He never came back!
He never came back to me!   20

  Calico Ban,
  The little Mice ran,
To be ready in time for tea,
  Flippity flup,
  They drank it all up,
  And danced in the cup, –

But they never came back to me!
  They never came back!
  They never came back!
They never came back to me!   30

  Calico Drum,
  The Grasshoppers come,
The Butterfly, Beetle, and Bee,
  Over the ground,
  Around and round,
  With a hop and a bound, –

But they never came back!
   They never came back!
   They never came back!
40   They never came back to me!

The Daddy Long-legs and the Fly

Once Mr Daddy Long-legs,
   Dressed in brown and gray,
Walked about upon the sands
   Upon a summer's day;
And there among the pebbles,
   When the wind was rather cold,
He met with Mr Floppy Fly,
   All dressed in blue and gold.
And as it was too soon to dine,
10   They drank some Periwinkle-wine,
And played an hour or two, or more,
At battlecock and shuttledore.

Said Mr Daddy Long-legs
   To Mr Floppy Fly,
'Why do you never come to court?
   I wish you'd tell me why.
All gold and shine, in dress so fine,
   You'd quite delight the court.
Why do you never go at all?
20   I really think you *ought*!
And if you went, you'd see such sights!

Such rugs! and jugs! and candle-lights!
And more than all, the King and Queen,
One in red, and one in green!'

'O Mr Daddy Long-legs,'
    Said Mr Floppy Fly,
'It's true I never go to court,
    And I will tell you why.
If I had six long legs like yours,
    At once I'd go to court!   30
But oh! I can't, because *my* legs
    Are so extremely short.
And I'm afraid the King and Queen
(One in red, and one in green)
Would say aloud, "You are not fit,
You Fly, to come to court to a bit!"'

'O Mr Daddy Long-legs,'
    Said Mr Floppy Fly,
'I wish you'd sing one little song!
    One mumbian melody!   40
You used to sing so awful well
    In former days gone by,
But now you never sing at all;
    I wish you'd tell me why:
For if you would, the silvery sound
Would please the shrimps and cockles round,
And all the crabs would gladly come
To hear you sing, "Ah, Hum di Hum!"'

Said Mr Daddy Long-legs,
    'I can never sing again!   50
And if you wish, I'll tell you why,
    Although it gives me pain.
For years I cannot hum a bit,
    Or sing the smallest song;
And this the dreadful reason is,
    My legs are grown too long!

My six long legs, all here and there,
Oppress my bosom with despair;
And if I stand, or lie, or sit,
60   I cannot sing one single bit!'

So Mr Daddy Long-legs
    And Mr Floppy Fly
Sat down in silence by the sea,
    And gazed upon the sky.
They said, 'This is a dreadful thing!
    The world has all gone wrong,
Since one has legs too short by half,
    The other much too long!
One never more can go to court,
70   Because his legs have grown too short;
The other cannot sing a song,
    Because his legs have grown too long!'

Then Mr Daddy Long-legs
    And Mr Floppy Fly
Rushed downward to the foamy sea
    With one sponge-taneous cry;
And there they found a little boat,
    Whose sails were pink and gray;
And off they sailed among the waves,
80   Far, and far away.
They sailed across the silent main,
And reached the great Gromboolian plain;
And there they play for evermore
At battlecock and shuttledore.

[Nonsense Cookery]

Extract from the *Nonsense Gazette*, for August, 1870.

Our readers will be interested in the following communications from our valued and learned contributor, Professor Bosh, whose labours in the fields of Culinary and Botanical science, are so well known to all the world. The first three Articles richly merit to be added to the Domestic cookery of every family; those which follow, claim the attention of all Botanists, and we are happy to be able through Dr Bosh's kindness to present our readers with Illustrations of his discoveries. All the new flowers are found in the valley of Verrikwier, near the lake of Oddgrow, and on the summit of the hill Orfeltugg.

THREE RECEIPTS FOR DOMESTIC COOKERY

TO MAKE AN AMBLONGUS PIE

Take 4 pounds (say 4 1/2 pounds) of fresh Amblongusses, and put them in a small pipkin.

Cover them with water and boil them for 8 hours incessantly, after which add 2 pints of new milk, and proceed to boil for 4 hours more.

When you have ascertained that the Amblongusses are quite soft, take them out and place them in a wide pan, taking care to shake them well previously.

Grate some nutmeg over the surface, and cover them carefully with powdered gingerbread, curry-powder, and a sufficient quantity of Cayenne pepper.

Remove the pan into the next room, and place it on the floor. Bring it back again, and let it simmer for three-quarters of an hour. Shake the pan violently till all the Amblongusses have become of a pale purple colour.

Then, having prepared the paste, insert the whole carefully, adding at the same time a small pigeon, 2 slices of beef, 4 cauliflowers, and any number of oysters.

Watch patiently till the crust begins to rise, and add a pinch of salt from time to time.

Serve up in a clean dish, and throw the whole out of the window as fast as possible.

TO MAKE CRUMBOBBLIOUS CUTLETS

Procure some strips of beef, and having cut them into the smallest possible slices, proceed to cut them still smaller, eight or perhaps nine times.

When the whole is thus minced, brush it up hastily with a new clothes-brush, and stir round rapidly and capriciously with a salt-spoon or a soup-ladle.

Place the whole in a saucepan, and remove it to a sunny place, – say the roof of the house if free from sparrows or other birds, – and leave it there for about a week.

At the end of that time add a little lavender, some oil of almonds, and a few herring-bones; and then cover the whole with 4 gallons of clarified crumbobblious sauce, when it will be ready for use.

Cut it into the shape of ordinary cutlets, and serve up in a clean tablecloth or dinner-napkin.

TO MAKE GOSKY PATTIES

Take a Pig, three or four years of age, and tie him by the off-hind leg to a post. Place 5 pounds of currants, 3 of sugar, 2 pecks of peas, 18 roast chestnuts, a candle, and six bushels of turnips, within his reach; if he eats these, constantly provide him with more.

Then procure some cream, some slices of Cheshire cheese, four quires of foolscap paper, and a packet of black pins. Work the whole into a paste, and spread it out to dry on a sheet of clean brown waterproof linen.

When the paste is perfectly dry, but not before, proceed to beat the Pig violently, with the handle of a large broom. If he squeals, beat him again.

Visit the paste and beat the Pig alternately for some days, and ascertain if at the end of that period the whole is about to turn into Gosky Patties.

If it does not then, it never will; and in that case the Pig may be let loose, and the whole process may be considered as finished.

[Nonsense Botany – 1]

Baccopipia Gracilis

Bottlephorkia Spoonifolia

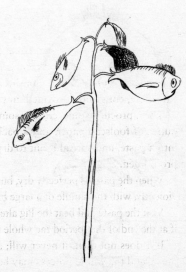

Cockatooca Superba

Fishia Marina

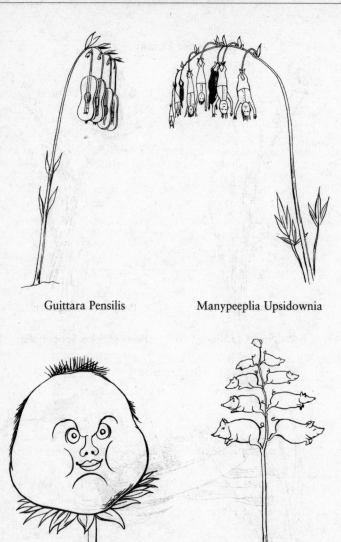

Guittara Pensilis

Manypeeplia Upsidownia

Phattfacia Stupenda

Piggiawiggia Pyramidalis

Plumbunnia Nutritiosa   Pollybirdia Singularis

The Jumblies

They went to sea in a Sieve, they did,
  In a Sieve they went to sea:
In spite of all their friends could say,
On a winter's morn, on a stormy day,
  In a Sieve they went to sea!
And when the Sieve turned round and round,

And every one cried, 'You'll all be drowned!'
They called aloud, 'Our Sieve ain't big,
But we don't care a button! we don't care a fig!
    In a Sieve we'll go to sea!'
        Far and few, far and few,
           Are the lands where the Jumblies live;
        Their heads are green, and their hands are blue,
           And they went to sea in a Sieve.

They sailed away in a Sieve, they did,
    In a Sieve they sailed so fast,
With only a beautiful pea-green veil
Tied with a riband by way of a sail,
    To a small tobacco-pipe mast;
And every one said, who saw them go,
'O won't they be soon upset, you know!
For the sky is dark, and the voyage is long,
And happen what may, it's extremely wrong
    In a Sieve to sail so fast!'
        Far and few, far and few,
           Are the lands where the Jumblies live;
        Their heads are green, and their hands are blue,
           And they went to sea in a Sieve.

The water it soon came in, it did,
    The water it soon came in;
So to keep them dry, they wrapped their feet
In a pinky paper all folded neat,
    And they fastened it down with a pin.
And they passed the night in a crockery-jar,
And each of them said, 'How wise we are!
Though the sky be dark, and the voyage be long,
Yet we never can think we were rash or wrong,
    While round in our Sieve we spin!'
        Far and few, far and few,
           Are the lands where the Jumblies live;
        Their heads are green, and their hands are blue,
           And they went to sea in a Sieve.

And all night long they sailed away;
   And when the sun went down,
They whistled and warbled a moony song
To the echoing sound of a coppery gong,
   In the shade of the mountains brown.
'O Timballo! How happy we are,
When we live in a sieve and a crockery-jar,
And all night long in the moonlight pale,   50
We sail away with a pea-green sail,
   In the shade of the mountains brown!'
      Far and few, far and few,
         Are the lands where the Jumblies live;
        Their heads are green, and their hands are blue,
         And they went to sea in a Sieve.

They sailed to the Western Sea, they did,
   To a land all covered with trees,
And they bought an Owl, and a useful Cart,
And a pound of Rice, and a Cranberry Tart,   60
   And a hive of silvery Bees.
And they bought a Pig, and some green Jack-daws,
And a lovely Monkey with lollipop paws,
And forty bottles of Ring-Bo-Ree,
   And no end of Stilton Cheese.
      Far and few, far and few,
         Are the lands where the Jumblies live;
        Their heads are green, and their hands are blue,
         And they went to sea in a Sieve.

And in twenty years they all came back,   70
   In twenty years or more,
And every one said, 'How tall they've grown!
For they've been to the Lakes, and the Torrible Zone,
   And the hills of the Chankly Bore!'
And they drank their health, and gave them a feast
Of dumplings made of beautiful yeast;
And every one said, 'If we only live,

We too will go to sea in a Sieve, –
To the hills of the Chankly Bore!'
    Far and few, far and few,
        Are the lands where the Jumblies live;
    Their heads are green, and their hands are blue,
        And they went to sea in a Sieve.

'The Absolutely Abstemious Ass'

THIS
ALPHABET
was made for
DAISY and ARTHUR TERRY
at
LA CERTOSA DEL PESIO
by their
ADOPTY DUNCLE,

Edward Lear.
August 31 1870

The Absolutely Abstemious Ass,
who resided in a Barrel, and only lived on
Soda Water and Pickled Cucumbers.

The Bountiful Beetle,
who always carried a Green Umbrella when it didn't rain,
and left it at home when it did.

The Comfortable Confidential Cow,
who sate in her Red Morocco Arm Chair and
toasted her own Bread at the parlour Fire.

The Dolomphious Duck,
who caught Spotted Frogs for her dinner
with a Runcible Spoon.

The Enthusiastic Elephant,
who ferried himself across the water with the
Kitchen Poker and a New pair of Ear-rings.

The Fizzgiggious Fish,
who always walked about upon Stilts
because he had no Legs.

The Goodnatured Grey Gull,
who carried the Old Owl, and his Crimson Carpet-bag
across the river, because he could not swim.

The Hasty Higgeldipiggledy Hen,
who went to market in a Blue Bonnet and Shawl,
and bought a Fish for her Supper.

The Inventive Indian,
who caught a Remarkable Rabbit in a
Stupendous Silver Spoon.

The Judicious Jubilant Jay,
who did up her Back Hair every morning with a Wreath of Roses,
Three Feathers, and a Gold Pin.

The Kicking Kangaroo,
who wore a Pale Pink Muslin Dress
with Blue Spots.

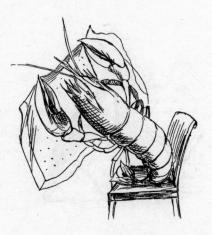

The Lively Learned Lobster,
who mended his own Clothes with
a Needle and Thread.

The Melodious Meritorious Mouse,
who played a Merry Minuet on the
Piano-forte.

The Nutritious Newt,
who purchased a Round Plum-pudding
for his Grand-daughter.

The Obsequious Ornamental Ostrich,
who wore Boots to keep his
Feet quite dry.

The Perpendicular Purple Polly,
who read the Newspaper and ate Parsnip Pie
with his Spectacles.

The Queer Querulous Quail,
who smoked a Pipe of Tobacco on the top of
a Tin Tea-kettle.

The Rural Runcible Raven,
who wore a White Wig and flew away
with the Carpet Broom.

The Scroobious Snake,
who always wore a Hat on his Head for
fear he should bite anybody.

The Tumultuous Tom-tommy Tortoise,
who beat a Drum all day long in the
middle of the Wilderness.

The Umbrageous Umbrella-maker,
whose Face nobody ever saw because it was
always covered by his Umbrella.

The Visibly Vicious Vulture,
who wrote some Verses to a Veal-cutlet in a
Volume bound in Vellum.

The Worrying Whizzing Wasp,
who stood on a Table, and played sweetly on a
Flute with a Morning Cap.

The Excellent Double-extra XX
imbibing King Xerxes, who lived a
long while ago.

The Yonghy-Bonghy-Bo,
whose Head was ever so much bigger than his
Body, and whose Hat was rather small.

The Zigzag Zealous Zebra,
who carried five Monkeys on his Back all
the way to Jellibolee.

'The Uncareful Cow, who walked about'

The Uncareful Cow, who walked about,
But took no care at all;
And so she bumped her silly head
Against a hard stone wall.
And when the Bump began to grow
Into a Horn, they said –
'There goes the Uncareful Cow, – who has
Three Horns upon her head!' –

And when the Bumpy Horn grew large,
'Uncareful Cow!' – they said –
'Here, take and hang this Camphor bottle
Upon your bumpy head! –
And with the Camphor rub the bump
Two hundred times a day.' –
And so she did – till bit by bit
She rubbed the Horn away.

10

[Creatures playing chequers]

The Nutcrackers and the Sugar-tongs

The Nutcrackers sate by a plate on the table,
    The Sugar-tongs sate by a plate at his side;
And the Nutcrackers said, 'Don't you wish we were able
    Along the blue hills and green meadows to ride?
Must we drag on this stupid existence for ever,
    So idle and weary, so full of remorse, –
While every one else takes his pleasure, and never
    Seems happy unless he is riding a horse?

'Don't you think we could ride without being instructed?
    Without any saddle, or bridle, or spur?
Our legs are so long, and so aptly constructed,
    I'm sure that an accident could not occur.
Let us all of a sudden hop down from the table,
    And hustle downstairs, and each jump on a horse!
Shall we try? Shall we go? Do you think we are able?'
    The Sugar-tongs answered distinctly, 'Of course!'

So down the long staircase they hopped in a minute,
    The Sugar-tongs snapped, and the Crackers said 'crack!'
The stable was open, the horses were in it;
    Each took out a pony, and jumped on his back.
The Cat in a fright scrambled out of the doorway,
    The Mice tumbled out of a bundle of hay,
The brown and white Rats, and the black ones from Norway,
    Screamed out, 'They are taking the horses away!'

The whole of the household was filled with amazement,
   The Cups and the Saucers danced madly about,
The Plates and the Dishes looked out of the casement,
   The Salt-cellar stood on his head with a shout,
The Spoons with a clatter looked out of the lattice,
   The Mustard-pot climbed up the Gooseberry Pies,   30
The Soup-ladle peeped through a heap of Veal Patties,
   And squeaked with a ladle-like scream of surprise.

The Frying-pan said, 'It's an awful delusion!'
   The Tea-kettle hissed and grew black in the face;
And they all rushed downstairs in the wildest confusion,
   To see the great Nutcracker–Sugar-tong race.
And out of the stable, with screamings and laughter,
   (Their ponies were cream-coloured, speckled with brown,)
The Nutcrackers first, and the Sugar-tongs after,
   Rode all round the yard, and then all round the town.   40

They rode through the street, and they rode by the station,
   They galloped away to the beautiful shore;
In silence they rode, and 'made no observation,'
   Save this: 'We will never go back any more!'
And still you might hear, till they rode out of hearing,
   The Sugar-tongs snap, and the Crackers say 'crack!'
Till far in the distance their forms disappearing,
   They faded away. – And they never came back!

Mr and Mrs Spikky Sparrow

On a little piece of wood,
Mr Spikky Sparrow stood;
Mrs Sparrow sate close by,
A-making of an insect pie,
For her little children five,
In the nest and all alive,
Singing with a cheerful smile
To amuse them all while,
    Twikky wikky wikky wee,
    Wikky bikky twikky tee,
    Spikky bikky bee!

Mrs Spikky Sparrow said,
'Spikky, Darling! in my head
Many thoughts of trouble come,
Like to flies upon a plum!
All last night, among the trees,
I heard you cough, I heard you sneeze;
And, thought I, it's come to that
Because he does not wear a hat!
    Chippy wippy sikky tee!
    Bikky wikky tikky mee!
    Spikky chippy wee!

'Not that you are growing old,
But the nights are growing cold.
No one stays out all night long
Without a hat: I'm sure it's wrong!'
Mr Spikky said, 'How kind,
Dear! you are, to speak your mind!
All your life I wish you luck!
You are! you are! a lovely duck!   30
  Witchy witchy witchy wee!
  Twitchy witchy witchy bee!
   Tikky tikky tee!

'I was also sad, and thinking, ·
When one day I saw you winking,
And I heard you sniffle-snuffle,
And I saw your feathers ruffle;
To myself I sadly said,
She's neuralgia in her head!
That dear head has nothing on it!   40
Ought she not to wear a bonnet?
  Witchy kitchy kitchy wee?
  Spikky wikky mikky bee?
   Chippy wippy chee?

'Let us both fly up to town!
There I'll buy you such a gown!
Which, completely in the fashion,
You shall tie a sky-blue sash on.
And a pair of slippers neat,
To fit your darling little feet,   50
So that you will look and feel
Quite galloobious and genteel!
  Jikky wikky bikky see,
  Chicky bikky wikky bee,
   Twicky witchy wee!'

So they both to London went,
Alighting on the Monument,
Whence they flew down swiftly – pop,
Into Moses' wholesale shop;
60   There they bought a hat and bonnet,
And a gown with spots upon it,
A satin sash of Cloxam blue,
And a pair of slippers too.
     Zikky wikky mikky bee,
     Witchy witchy mitchy kee,
       Sikky tikky wee!

Then when so completely drest,
Back they flew, and reached their nest.
Their children cried, 'O Ma and Pa!
70   How truly beautiful you are!'
Said they, 'We trust that cold or pain
We shall never feel again!
While, perched on tree, or house, or steeple,
We now shall look like other people.
     Witchy witchy witchy wee,
     Twikky mikky bikky bee,
       Zikky sikky tee!'

The Table and the Chair

Said the Table to the Chair,
'You can hardly be aware,
How I suffer from the heat,
And from chilblains on my feet!
If we took a little walk,
We might have a little talk!
Pray let us take the air!'
Said the Table to the Chair.

Said the Chair unto the Table,
'Now you *know* we are not able!   10
How foolishly you talk,
When you know we *cannot* walk!'
Said the Table, with a sigh,
'It can do no harm to try,
I've as many legs as you,
Why can't we walk on two?'

So they both went slowly down,
And walked about the town
With a cheerful bumpy sound,
As they toddled round and round.   20
And everybody cried,
As they hastened to their side,

'See! the Table and the Chair,
Have come out to take the air!'

But in going down an alley,
To a castle in the valley,
They completely lost their way,
And wandered all the day,
Till, to see them safely back,
30   They paid a Ducky-quack,
And a Beetle, and a Mouse,
Who took them to their house.

Then they whispered to each other,
'O delightful little brother!
What a lovely walk we've taken!
Let us dine on Beans and Bacon!'
So the Ducky, and the leetle
Browny-Mousy and the Beetle
Dined, and danced upon their heads
40   Till they toddled to their beds.

'A was once an apple-pie'

A was once an apple-pie,
  Pidy
  Widy
  Tidy
  Pidy
Nice insidy
Apple-Pie!

B

b

B was once a little bear,
  Beary
  Wary
  Hairy
  Beary
Taky cary
Little Bear!

C

C

C was once a little cake,
   Caky
   Baky
   Maky
   Caky
Taky caky
Little Cake!

D

d

D was once a little doll,
   Dolly
   Molly
   Polly
   Nolly
Nursy dolly
Little Doll!

E

e

E was once a little eel,
  Eely
  Weely
  Peely
  Eely
Twirly-tweely
Little Eel!

F

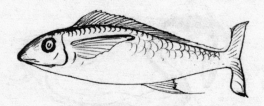

f

F was once a little fish,
  Fishy
  Wishy
  Squishy
  Fishy
In a dishy
Little Fish!

G was once a little goose,
  Goosy
  Moosy
  Boosey
  Goosey
Waddly-woosy
Little Goose!

h

H was once a little hen,
  Henny
  Chenny
  Tenny
  Henny
Eggsy-any
Little Hen?

I

i

I was once a bottle of ink,
  Inky
  Dinky
  Thinky
  Inky
Blacky minky
Bottle of Ink!

J was once a jar of jam,
  Jammy
  Mammy
  Clammy
  Jammy
Sweety-swammy
Jar of Jam!

K

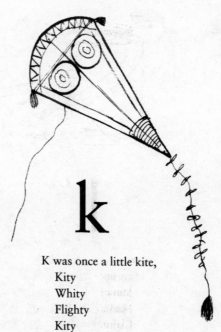

k

K was once a little kite,
  Kity
  Whity
  Flighty
  Kity
Out of sighty
Little Kite!

1

L was once a little lark,
   Larky
   Marky
   Harky
   Larky
In the parky
Little Lark!

M

m

M was once a little mouse,
  Mousey
  Bousey
  Sousy
  Mousy
In the housy
Little Mouse!

N

n

N was once a little needle,
  Needly
  Tweedly
  Threedly
  Needly
Wisky-wheedly
Little Needle!

O

O

O was once a little owl,
    Owly
    Prowly
    Howly
    Owly
Browny fowly
Little Owl!

P

p

P was once a little pump,
   Pumpy
   Slumpy
   Flumpy
   Pumpy
Dumpy thumpy
Little Pump!

Q

q

Q was once a little quail,
   Quaily
   Faily
   Daily
   Quaily
Stumpy-taily
Little Quail!

R

r

R was once a little rose,
   Rosy
   Posy
   Nosy
   Rosy
Blows-y grows-y
Little Rose!

S

S

S was once a little shrimp,
    Shrimpy
    Nimpy
    Flimpy
    Shrimpy
Jumpy-jimpy
Little Shrimp!

T

t

T was once a little thrush,
   Thrushy
   Hushy
   Bushy
   Thrushy
Flitty-flushy
Little Thrush!

U

u

U was once a little urn,
   Urny
   Burny
   Turny
   Urny
Bubbly-burny
Little Urn!

V

V

V was once a little vine,
   Viny
   Winy
   Twiny
   Viny
Twisty-twiny
Little Vine!

W

W

W was once a whale,
  Whaly
  Scaly
  Shaly
  Whaly
Tumbly-taily
Mighty Whale!

X

X

X was once a great king Xerxes,
  Xerxy
  Perxy
  Turxy
  Xerxy
Linxy-lurxy
Great King Xerxes!

Y was once a little yew,
  Yewdy
  Fewdy
  Crudy
  Yewdy
Growdy grewdy
Little Yew!

Z

Z

Z was once a piece of zinc,
   Tinky
   Winky
   Blinky
   Tinky
Tinkly minky
Piece of Zinc!

'A was an Area Arch'

Papa he said, 'My little Boy!
   My little Boy so dear!
This Alphabet was made for you,
   By Mr Edward Lear.
And should you ever meet with him,
   This is his picture here.'
Papa he said, – 'This really does
   Resemble,

Edward Lear.'

A

A was an Area Arch,
Where washerwomen sat;
They made a lot of lovely starch
To starch Papa's cravat.

B

B was a Bottle Blue,
Which was not very small;
Papa he filled it full of beer,
And then he drank it all.

C

C was Papa's gray Cat,
Who caught a squeaky Mouse;
She pulled him by his twirly tail
All about the house.

D

D was Papa's white Duck,
Who had a curly tail;
One day it ate a great fat frog,
Besides a leetle snail.

E

E was a little Egg,
Upon the breakfast table;
Papa came in and ate it up
As fast as he was able.

F

F was a little Fish,
Cook in the river took it;
Papa said, 'Cook! Cook! bring a dish!
And Cook! be quick and cook it!'

G

G was Papa's new Gun,
He put it in a box;
And then he went and bought a bun,
And walked about the docks.

H

H was Papa's new Hat,
He wore it on his head;
Outside it was completely black,
But inside it was red.

I

I was an Inkstand new,
Papa he likes to use it;
He keeps it in his pocket now,
For fear that he should lose it.

J

J was some Apple Jam,
Of which Papa ate part,
But all the rest he took away,
And stuffed into a tart.

K

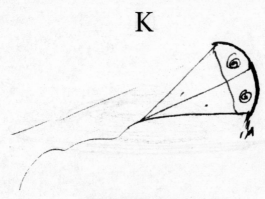

K was a great new Kite,
Papa he saw it fly
Above a thousand chimney pots,
And all about the sky.

L

L was a fine new Lamp,
But when the wick was lit,
Papa he said, 'This light ain't good!
I cannot read a bit!'

M

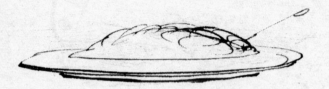

M was a dish of Mince,
It looked so good to eat!
Papa, he quickly ate it up,
And said, 'This is a treat!'

N

N was a Nut that grew
High up upon a tree;
Papa, who could not reach it, said,
'That's much too high for me!'

O

O was an Owl who flew
All in the dark away;
Papa said, 'What an owl you are!
Why don't you fly by day!'

P

P was a little Pig,
Went out to take a walk;
Papa he said, 'If Piggy dead,
He'd all turn into pork!'

Q

Q was a Quince that hung
Upon a garden tree;
Papa he brought it with him home,
And ate it with his tea.

R

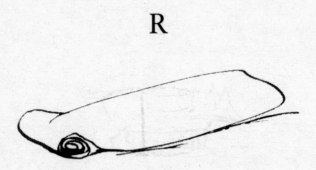

R was a Railway Rug,
Extremely large and warm;
Papa he wrapped it round his head
In a most dreadful storm.

S

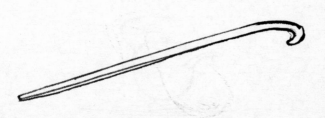

S was Papa's new Stick,
Papa's new thumping Stick,
To thump extremely wicked boys,
Because it was so thick.

T

T was a Tumbler full
Of punch all hot and good;
Papa he drank it up, when in
The middle of a wood.

U

U was a silver Urn,
Full of hot scalding water;
Papa said, 'If that Urn were mine,
I'd give it to my daughter!'

V

V was a Villain; once
He stole a piece of beef;
Papa he said, 'O! dreadful man!
That Villain is a thief!'

W

W was a Watch of gold,
It told the time of day,
So that Papa knew when to come,
And when to go away.

X

X was King Xerxes, whom
Papa much wished to know;
But this he could not do, because
Xerxes died long ago.

Y

Y was a Youth, who kicked
And screamed and cried like mad;
Papa he said, 'Your conduct is
Abominably bad!'

Z

Z was a Zebra striped
And streaked with lines of black;
Papa said once, he thought he'd like
A ride upon his back.

[Mr Lear receives a letter from Marianne North]

Mr Lear refuses to pay for a Letter insufficiently stamped and sends it away.

Mr Lear remembers that the handwriting is Miss North's, and stamps with late remorse and rage.

Mr Lear executes a rapid Stampede to the Post Office.

Mr Lear delivers an extampary and affecting discourse to obtain the Letter.

Mr Lear stamps and dances for joy on securing Miss North's letter.

Mr and Mrs Discobbolos

Mr and Mrs Discobbolos
    Climbed to the top of a wall,
   And they sate to watch the sunset sky
   And to hear the Nupiter Piffkin cry
    And the Biscuit Buffalo call.
They took up a roll and some Camomile tea,
And both were as happy as happy could be –
    Till Mrs Discobbolos said –
    'Oh! W! X! Y! Z!
    It has just come into my head –   10
Suppose we should happen to fall!!!!!
           Darling Mr Discobbolos!

'Suppose we should fall down flumpetty
    Just like pieces of stone!
  On to the thorns, – or into the moat!
   What would become of your new green coat?
    And might you not break a bone?
It never occurred to me before –
That perhaps we shall never go down any more!'
    And Mrs Discobbolos said –   20
    'Oh! W! X! Y! Z!
    What put it into your head
To climb up this wall? – my own
           Darling Mr Discobbolos?'

Mr Discobbolos answered, –
    'At first it gave me pain, –
  And I felt my ears turn perfectly pink
   When your exclamation made me think
    We might never get down again!
But now I believe it is wiser far   30
To remain for ever just where we are.' –
    And Mr Discobbolos said,
    'Oh! W! X! Y! Z!

It is just come into my head –
– We shall never go down again –
Dearest Mrs Discobbolos!'

So Mr and Mrs Discobbolos
Stood up, and began to sing,
'Far away from hurry and strife
Here we will pass the rest of life,
Ding a dong, ding dong, ding!
We want no knives nor forks nor chairs,
No tables nor carpets nor household cares,
From worry of life we've fled –
Oh! W! X! Y! Z!
There's no more trouble ahead,
Sorrow or any such thing –
For Mr and Mrs Discobbolos!'

The Courtship of the Yonghy-Bonghy-Bò

On the Coast of Coromandel
   Where the early pumpkins blow,
     In the middle of the woods
     Lived the Yonghy-Bonghy-Bò.
Two old chairs, and half a candle, –
One old jug without a handle, –
     These were all his worldly goods,
     In the middle of the woods,
     These were all the worldly goods,
     Of the Yonghy-Bonghy-Bò,
     Of the Yonghy-Bonghy-Bò.

Once, among the Bong-trees walking
   Where the early pumpkins blow,
     To a little heap of stones
     Came the Yonghy-Bonghy-Bò.
There he heard a Lady talking,
To some milk-white Hens of Dorking, –
     "Tis the Lady Jingly Jones!
     On that little heap of stones
     Sits the Lady Jingly Jones!'
     Said the Yonghy-Bonghy-Bò,
     Said the Yonghy-Bonghy-Bò.

'Lady Jingly! Lady Jingly!
    Sitting where the pumpkins blow,
        Will you come and be my wife?'
    Said the Yonghy-Bonghy-Bò.
'I am tired of living singly, –
On this coast so wild and shingly, –
        I'm a-weary of my life;
        If you'll come and be my wife,   30
        Quite serene would be my life!' –
    Said the Yonghy-Bonghy-Bò,
    Said the Yonghy-Bonghy-Bò.

'On this Coast of Coromandel,
    Shrimps and watercresses grow,
        Prawns are plentiful and cheap,'
    Said the Yonghy-Bonghy-Bò.
'You shall have my chairs and candle,
And my jug without a handle! –
        Gaze upon the rolling deep   40
        (Fish is plentiful and cheap;)
        As the sea, my love is deep!'
    Said the Yonghy-Bonghy-Bò,
    Said the Yonghy-Bonghy-Bò.

Lady Jingly answered sadly,
    And her tears began to flow, –
        'Your proposal comes too late,
    Mr Yonghy-Bonghy-Bò!
I would be your wife most gladly!'
(Here she twirled her fingers madly,)   50
        'But in England I've a mate!
        Yes! you've asked me far too late,
        For in England I've a mate,
    Mr Yonghy-Bonghy-Bò!
    Mr Yonghy-Bonghy-Bò!'

'Mr Jones – (his name is Handel, –
  Handel Jones, Esquire, & Co.)
    Dorking fowls delights to send,
  Mr Yonghy-Bonghy-Bò!
Keep, oh! keep your chairs and candle,
And your jug without a handle, –
    I can merely be your friend!
    – Should my Jones more Dorkings send,
    I will give you three, my friend!
  Mr Yonghy-Bonghy-Bò!
  Mr Yonghy-Bonghy-Bò!

'Though you've such a tiny body,
  And your head so large doth grow, –
    Though your hat may blow away,
  Mr Yonghy-Bonghy-Bò!
Though you're such a Hoddy Doddy –
Yet I wished that I could modi-
    fy the words I needs must say!
    Will you please to go away?
    That is all I have to say –
  Mr Yonghy-Bonghy-Bò!
  Mr Yonghy-Bonghy-Bò!'

Down the slippery slopes of Myrtle,
  Where the early pumpkins blow,
    To the calm and silent sea
  Fled the Yonghy-Bonghy-Bò.
There, beyond the Bay of Gurtle,
Lay a large and lively Turtle; –
    'You're the Cove,' he said, 'for me;
    On your back beyond the sea,
    Turtle, you shall carry me!'
  Said the Yonghy-Bonghy-Bò,
  Said the Yonghy-Bonghy-Bò.

Through the silent-roaring ocean
  Did the Turtle swiftly go;
    Holding fast upon his shell
  Rode the Yonghy-Bonghy-Bò.
With a sad primæval motion
Towards the sunset isles of Boshen
    Still the Turtle bore him well.
    Holding fast upon his shell,
    'Lady Jingly Jones, farewell!'
  Said the Yonghy-Bonghy-Bò,
  Said the Yonghy-Bonghy-Bò.

From the Coast of Coromandel,
  Did that Lady never go;
    On that heap of stones she mourns
  For the Yonghy-Bonghy-Bò.
On that Coast of Coromandel,
In his jug without a handle,
    Still she weeps, and daily moans;
    On that little heap of stones
    To her Dorking Hens she moans,
  For the Yonghy-Bonghy-Bò,
  For the Yonghy-Bonghy-Bò.

[Limericks published in *More Nonsense*]

There was a Young Person of Bantry,
Who frequently slept in the pantry;
When disturbed by the mice, she appeased them with rice
That judicious Young Person of Bantry.

There was an Old Man at a Junction,
Whose feelings were wrung with compunction;
When they said, 'The Train's gone!' he exclaimed 'How forlorn,'
But remained on the rails of the Junction.

There was an Old Man, who when little,
Fell casually into a kettle;
But, growing too stout, he could never get out,
So he passed all his life in that kettle.

There was an Old Man whose despair
Induced him to purchase a hare;
Whereon one fine day, he rode wholly away,
Which partly assuaged his despair.

There was an Old Person of Minety,
Who purchased five hundred and ninety
Large apples and pears, which he threw unawares,
At the heads of the people of Minety.

There was an Old Man of Thermopylæ,
Who never did anything properly;
But they said, 'If you choose to boil eggs in your shoes,
You shall never remain in Thermopylæ.'

There was an Old Person of Deal,
Who in walking used only his heel;
When they said, 'Tell us why?' – he made no reply;
That mysterious Old Person of Deal.

There was an Old Man on the Humber,
Who dined on a cake of Burnt Umber;
When he said, 'It's enough!' – they only said, 'Stuff!
You amazing Old Man on the Humber!'

There was an Old Man of Blackheath,
Whose head was adorned with a wreath
Of lobsters and spice, pickled onions and mice,
That uncommon Old Man of Blackheath.

There was an Old Man of Toulouse,
Who purchased a new pair of shoes;
When they asked, 'Are they pleasant?' he said, 'Not at present!'
That turbid Old Man of Toulouse.

There was an Old Person in black,
A Grasshopper jumped on his back;
When it chirped in his ear, he was smitten with fear,
That helpless Old Person in black.

There was an Old Man in a barge,
Whose nose was exceedingly large;
But in fishing by night, it supported a light,
Which helped that Old Man in a barge.

There was an Old Man of Dunrose,
A parrot seized hold of his nose;
When he grew melancholy, they said, 'His name's Polly,'
Which soothed that Old Man of Dunrose.

There was an Old Person of Bromley,
Whose ways were not cheerful or comely;
He sate in the dust, eating spiders and crust,
That unpleasing Old Person of Bromley.

There was an Old Man of Dunluce,
Who went out to sea on a goose;
When he'd gone out a mile, he observ'd with a smile,
'It is time to return to Dunluce.'

There was an Old Person of Pinner,
As thin as a lath, if not thinner;
They dressed him in white, and roll'd him up tight,
That elastic Old Person of Pinner.

There was an Old Man in a Marsh,
Whose manners were futile and harsh;
He sate on a log, and sang songs to a frog,
That instructive Old Man in a Marsh.

There was an Old Man of Dee-side,
Whose hat was exceedingly wide;
But he said, 'Do not fail, if it happened to hail,
To come under my hat at Dee-side!'

There was an Old Person of Bree,
Who frequented the depths of the sea;
She nurs'd the small fishes, and washed all the dishes,
And swam back again into Bree.

There was a Young Person in green,
Who seldom was fit to be seen;
She wore a long shawl, over bonnet and all,
Which envelloped that Person in green.

There was an Old Person of Wick,
Who said, 'Tick-a-Tick, Tick-a-Tick,
Chickabee, Chickabaw.' And he said, nothing more,
That laconic Old Person of Wick.

There was an Old Man at a Station,
Who made a promiscuous oration;
But they said, 'Take some snuff! – You have talk'd quite enough,
You afflicting Old Man at a Station!'

There was an Old Man of Three Bridges,
Whose mind was distracted by midges;
He sate on a wheel, eating underdone veal,
Which relieved that Old Man of Three Bridges.

There was an Old Person of Woking,
Whose mind was perverse and provoking;
He sate on a rail, with his head in a pail,
That illusive Old Person of Woking.

There was an Old Person of Fife,
Who was greatly disgusted with life;
They sang him a ballad, and fed him on salad,
Which cured that Old Person of Fife.

There was an Old Person of Shields,
Who frequented the vallies and fields;
All the mice and the cats, and the snakes and the rats,
Followed after that Person of Shields.

There was an Old Person of China,
Whose daughters were Jiska and Dinah,
Amelia and Fluffy, Olivia and Chuffy,
And all of them settled in China.

There was an Old Man of the Dargle,
Who purchased six barrels of Gargle;
For he said, 'I'll sit still, and will roll them downhill,
For the fish in the depths of the Dargle.'

There was an Old Man who screamed out
Whenever they knocked him about;
So they took off his boots, and fed him with fruits,
And continued to knock him about.

There was an Old Person of Brill,
Who purchased a shirt with a frill;
But they said, 'Don't you wish you mayn't look like a fish,
You obsequious Old Person of Brill?'

There was an Old Person of Slough,
Who danced at the end of a bough;
But they said, 'If you sneeze, you might damage the trees,
You imprudent Old Person of Slough.'

There was a Young Person in red,
Who carefully covered her head
With a bonnet of leather, and three lines of feather,
Besides some long ribands of red.

There was a Young Person in pink,
Who called out for something to drink;
But they said, 'O my daughter, there's nothing but water!'
Which vexed that Young Person in pink.

There was a Young Lady in white,
Who looked out at the depths of the night;
But the birds of the air, filled her heart with despair,
And oppressed that Young Lady in white.

There was an Old Man of Hong Kong,
Who never did anything wrong;
He lay on his back, with his head in a sack,
That innocuous Old Man of Hong Kong.

There was an Old Person of Putney,
Whose food was roast spiders and chutney,
Which he took with his tea, within sight of the sea,
That romantic Old Person of Putney.

There was an Old Lady of France,
Who taught little ducklings to dance;
When she said, 'Tick-a-tack!' – they only said, 'Quack!'
Which grieved that Old Lady of France.

There was a Young Lady in blue,
Who said, 'Is it you? Is it you?'
When they said, 'Yes, it is,' – she replied only, 'Whizz!'
That ungracious Young Lady in blue.

There was an Old Man in a garden,
Who always begged everyone's pardon;
When they asked him, 'What for?' – he replied, 'You're a bore!
And I trust you'll go out of my garden.'

There was an Old Person of Loo,
Who said, 'What on earth shall I do?'
When they said, 'Go away!' – she continued to stay,
That vexatious Old Person of Loo.

There was an Old Person of Pisa,
Whose daughters did nothing to please her;
She dressed them in gray, and banged them all day,
Round the walls of the city of Pisa.

There was an Old Person of Florence,
Who held mutton chops in abhorrence;
He purchased a Bustard, and fried him in Mustard,
Which choked that Old Person of Florence.

There was an Old Person of Sheen,
Whose expression was calm and serene;
He sate in the water, and drank bottled porter,
That placid Old Person of Sheen.

There was an Old Person of Ware,
Who rode on the back of a bear;
When they ask'd, 'Does it trot?' – he said, 'Certainly not!
He's a Moppsikon Floppsikon Bear!'

There was an Old Person of Dean,
Who dined on one pea and one bean;
For he said, 'More than that would make me too fat,'
That cautious Old Person of Dean.

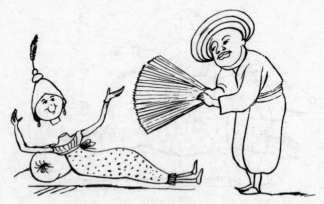

There was a Young Person of Janina,
Whose uncle was always a-fanning her;
When he fanned off her head, she smiled sweetly, and said,
'You propitious Old Person of Janina!'

There was an Old Person of Down,
Whose face was adorned with a frown;
When he opened the door, for one minute or more,
He alarmed all the people of Down.

There was an Old Person of Cassel,
Whose nose finished off in a tassel;
But they call'd out, 'Oh well! – don't it look like a bell!'
Which perplexed that Old Person of Cassel.

There was an Old Man of Cashmere,
Whose movements were scroobious and queer;
Being slender and tall, he looked over a wall,
And perceived two fat ducks of Cashmere.

There was an Old Person of Hove,
Who frequented the depths of a grove
Where he studied his books, with the wrens and the rooks,
That tranquil Old Person of Hove.

There was an Old Man of Spithead,
Who opened the window, and said, –
'Fil-jomble, fil-jumble, fil-rumble-come-tumble!'
That doubtful Old Man of Spithead.

There was an Old Man on the Border,
Who lived in the utmost disorder;
He danced with the cat, and made tea in his hat,
Which vexed all the folks on the Border.

There was an Old Person of Dundalk,
Who tried to teach fishes to walk;
When they tumbled down dead, he grew weary, and said,
'I had better go back to Dundalk!'

There was an Old Man of Dumbree,
Who taught little owls to drink tea;
For he said, 'To eat mice is not proper or nice',
That amiable Man of Dumbree.

There was an Old Person of Jodd,
Whose ways were perplexing and odd;
She purchased a whistle, and sate on a thistle,
And squeaked to the people of Jodd.

There was an Old Person of Shoreham,
Whose habits were marked by decorum;
He bought an Umbrella, and sate in the cellar,
Which pleased all the people of Shoreham.

There was an Old Man whose remorse,
Induced him to drink Caper Sauce;
For he said, 'If mixed up with some cold claret-cup,
It will certainly soothe your remorse!'

There was an Old Person of Wilts,
Who constantly walked upon stilts;
He wreathed them with lilies and daffy-down-dillies,
That elegant Person of Wilts.

There was an Old Person of Newry,
Whose manners were tinctured with fury;
He tore all the rugs, and broke all the jugs
Within twenty miles' distance of Newry.

There was an Old Person of Pett,
Who was partly consumed by regret;
He sate in a cart, and ate cold apple tart,
Which relieved that Old Person of Pett.

There was an Old Man of Port Grigor,
Whose actions were noted for vigour;
He stood on his head, till his waistcoat turned red,
That eclectic Old Man of Port Grigor.

There was an Old Person of Bar,
Who passed all her life in a jar,
Which she painted pea-green, to appear more serene,
That placid Old Person of Bar.

There was an Old Man of West Dumpet,
Who possessed a large nose like a trumpet;
When he blew it aloud, it astonished the crowd,
And was heard through the whole of West Dumpet.

There was an Old Person of Grange,
Whose manners were scroobious and strange;
He sailed to St Blubb, in a waterproof tub,
That aquatic Old Person of Grange.

There was an Old Person of Nice,
Whose associates were usually Geese;
They walked out together, in all sorts of weather,
That affable Person of Nice!

There was a Young Person of Kew,
Whose virtues and vices were few;
But with blameable haste, she devoured some hot paste,
Which destroyed that Young Person of Kew.

There was an Old Person of Sark,
Who made an unpleasant remark;
But they said, 'Don't you see what a brute you must be!
You obnoxious Old Person of Sark.'

There was an Old Person of Filey,
Of whom his acquaintance spoke highly;
He danced perfectly well, to the sound of a bell,
And delighted the people of Filey.

There was an Old Man of El Hums,
Who lived upon nothing but crumbs,
Which he picked off the ground, with the other birds round,
In the roads and the lanes of El Hums.

There was an Old Man of Dunblane,
Who greatly resembled a crane;
But they said, – 'Is it wrong, since your legs are so long,
To request you won't stay in Dunblane?'

There was an Old Person of Hyde,
Who walked by the shore with his bride,
Till a Crab who came near, fill'd their bosoms with fear,
And they said, 'Would we'd never left Hyde!'

There was an Old Man of Ancona,
Who found a small dog with no owner,
Which he took up and down all the streets of the town,
That anxious Old Man of Ancona.

There was an Old Person of Rimini,
Who said, 'Gracious! Goodness! O Gimini!'
When they said, 'Please be still!' she ran down a hill,
And was never more heard of at Rimini.

There was an Old Person of Cannes,
Who purchased three fowls and a fan;
Those she placed on a stool, and to make them feel cool
She constantly fanned them at Cannes.

There was an Old Person of Bude,
Whose deportment was vicious and crude;
He wore a large ruff, of pale straw-colored stuff,
Which perplexed all the people of Bude.

There was an Old Person of Ickley,
Who could not abide to ride quickly;
He rode to Karnak, on a tortoise's back,
That moony Old Person of Ickley.

There was an Old Person of Barnes,
Whose garments were covered with darns;
But they said, 'Without doubt, you will soon wear them out,
You luminous Person of Barnes!'

There was an Old Person of Blythe,
Who cut up his meat with a scythe;
When they said, 'Well! I never!' – he cried, 'Scythes for ever!'
That lively Old Person of Blythe.

There was an Old Person of Ealing,
Who was wholly devoid of good feeling;
He drove a small gig, with three Owls and a Pig,
Which distressed all the people of Ealing.

There was an Old Person of Bray,
Who sang through the whole of the day
To his ducks and his pigs, whom he fed upon figs,
That valuable Person of Bray.

There was an Old Person of Bow,
Whom nobody happened to know;
So they gave him some soap, and said, coldly, 'We hope
You will go back directly to Bow!'

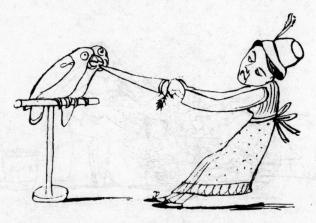

There was an Old Person in gray,
Whose feelings were tinged with dismay;
She purchased two parrots, and fed them with carrots,
Which pleased that Old Person in gray.

There was an Old Person of Crowle,
Who lived in the nest of an owl;
When they screamed in the nest, he screamed out with the rest,
That depressing Old Person of Crowle.

There was an Old Person of Brigg,
Who purchased no end of a wig,
So that only his nose, and the end of his toes,
Could be seen when he walked about Brigg.

There was a Young Lady of Greenwich,
Whose garments were border'd with Spinach;
But a large spotty Calf, bit her shawl quite in half,
Which alarmed that Young Lady of Greenwich.

There was an Old Person of Rye,
Who went up to town on a fly;
But they said, 'If you cough, you are safe to fall off!
You abstemious Old Person of Rye!'

There was an Old Man of Messina,
Whose daughter was named Opsibeena;
She wore a small wig, and rode out on a pig,
To the perfect delight of Messina.

There was a Young Lady whose nose,
Continually prospers and grows;
When it grew out of sight, she exclaimed in a fright,
'Oh! Farewell to the end of my nose!'

There was an Old Person of Sestri,
Who sate himself down in the vestry;
When they said, 'You are wrong!' – he merely said, 'Bong!'
That repulsive Old Person of Sestri.

There was an Old Man in a tree,
Whose whiskers were lovely to see;
But the birds of the air pluck'd them perfectly bare,
To make themselves nests in that tree.

There was a Young Lady of Corsica,
Who purchased a little brown saucy-cur
Which she fed upon ham, and hot raspberry jam,
That expensive Young Lady of Corsica.

There was a Young Lady of Firle,
Whose hair was addicted to curl;
It curled up a tree, and all over the sea,
That expansive Young Lady of Firle.

There was an Old Lady of Winchelsea,
Who said, 'If you needle or pin shall see
On the floor of my room, sweep it up with the broom!' –
That exhaustive Old Lady of Winchelsea!

There was a Young Person whose history
Was always considered a mystery;
She sate in a ditch, although no one knew which,
And composed a small treatise on history.

There was an Old Man of Boulak,
Who sate on a Crocodile's back;
But they said, 'Tow'rds the night, he may probably bite,
Which might vex you, Old Man of Boulak!'

There was an Old Man of Ibreem,
Who suddenly threaten'd to scream;
But they said, 'If you do, we will thump you quite blue,
You disgusting Old Man of Ibreem!'

There was an Old Person of Stroud,
Who was horribly jammed in a crowd;
Some she slew with a kick, some she scrunched with a stick,
That impulsive Old Person of Stroud.

There was an Old Man of Thames Ditton,
Who called out for something to sit on;
But they brought him a hat, and said, 'Sit upon that,
You abruptious Old Man of Thames Ditton!'

There was an Old Person of Skye,
Who waltz'd with a Bluebottle fly;
They buzz'd a sweet tune, to the light of the moon,
And entranced all the people of Skye.

There was a Young Person of Ayr,
Whose head was remarkably square;
On the top, in fine weather, she wore a gold feather,
Which dazzled the people of Ayr.

[Extra limericks prepared for *More Nonsense*]

There was an Old Person of Brussels,
Who lived upon Brandy and Mussels;
When he rushed through the town, he knocked most people down,
Which distressed all the people of Brussels.

There was an Old Man of the hills,
Who lived upon Syrup of Squills;
Which he drank all night long, to the sound of a gong,
That persistent Old Man of the hills.

There was an Old Person of Twickenham,
Who whipped his four horses to quicken 'em;
When they stood on one leg, he said faintly, 'I beg
We may go back directly to Twickenham.'

There was an Old Person of Bradley,
Who sang all so loudly and sadly;
With a poker and tongs, he beat time to his songs,
That melodious Old Person of Bradley.

There was an Old Man of Carlisle,
Who was left in a desolate isle;
Where he fed upon cakes, and lived wholly with snakes,
Who danced with that Man of Carlisle.

There was an Old Person of Diss,
Who said, 'It is this! It is this!'
When they said, 'What? or which?' – he jumped into a ditch,
Which absorbed that Old Person of Diss.

There was an Old Person of Harrow,
Who bought a mahogany barrow;
For he said to his wife, 'You're the joy of my life!
And I'll wheel you all day in this barrow!'

There was an Old Person of Cheam,
Who said, 'It is just like a dream,
When I play on the drum, and wear rings on my thumb
In the beautiful meadows of Cheam!'

There was an Old Man of Girgenti,
Who lived in profusion and plenty;
He lay on two chairs, and ate thousands of pears,
That susceptible Man of Girgenti.

[Nonsense Botany – 2]

Barkia Howlaloudia

Enkoopia Chickabiddia

Jinglia Tinkettlia

Nasticreechia Krorluppia

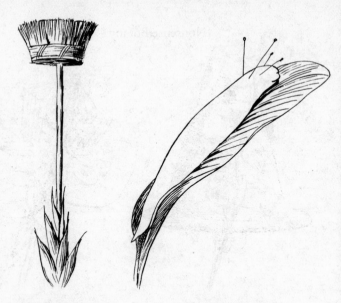

Arthbroomia Rigida   Sophtsluggia Glutinosa

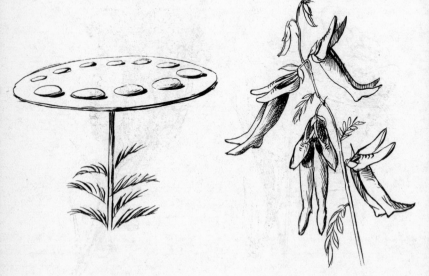

Minspysia Deliciosa   Shoebootia Utilis

Stunnia Dinnerbellia

Tickia Orologica

Washtubbia Circularis

Tigerlillia Terribilis

'Cold are the crabs that crawl on yonder hill'

Cold are the crabs that crawl on yonder hill,
Colder the cucumbers that grow beneath
And colder still the brazen chops that wreath
The tedious gloom of philosophic pills!
For when the tardy film of nectar fills
The ample bowls of demons and of men,
There lurks the feeble mouse, the homely hen,
And there the Porcupine with all her quills.
Yet much remains; – to weave a solemn strain
That lingering sadly – slowly dies away,
Daily departing with departing day
A pea-green gamut on a distant plain.
Where wily walruses in congress meet –
Such such is life –
Where early buffaloes in congress meet
Than salt more salt, than sugar still more sweet,
And pearly centipedes adjust their feet
Where buffaloes bewail the loss of soap
Where frantic walruses in clouds elope,
And early pipkins bid adiew to hope.

The Scroobious Pip

The Scroobious Pip went out one day
When the grass was green, and the sky was gray,
Then all the beasts in the world came round
When the Scroobious Pip sate down on the ground.
The Cats and the Dog and the Kangaroo,
The Sheep and the Cow and the Guinea Pig too –
The Wolf he howled, the Horse he neighed,
The little Pig squeaked and the Donkey brayed,
And when the Lion began to roar
There never was heard such a noise before,   10
And every beast he stood on the tip
Of his toes to look at the Scroobious Pip.

At last they said to the Fox – 'By far
You're the wisest beast – you know you are!
Go close to the Scroobious Pip and say,
"Tell us all about yourself we pray! –
For as yet we can't make out in the least
If you're Fish or Insect, or Bird or Beast."'

The Scroobious Pip looked vaguely round
And sang these words with a rumbling sound –
    'Chippetty Flip – Flippetty Chip –
    My only name is the Scroobious Pip.'

The Scroobious Pip from the top of a tree
Saw the distant Jellybolee, –
And all the birds in the world came there,
Flying in crowds all through the air.
The Vulture and Eagle – the Cock and the Hen,
The Ostrich, the Turkey, the Snipe and Wren,
The Parrot chattered, the Blackbird sung,
And the Owl looked wise but held his tongue,
And when the Peacock began to scream,
The hullabaloo was quite extreme.
And every bird he fluttered the tip
Of his wing as he stared at the Scroobious Pip.

At last they said to the Owl, – 'By far
You're wisest Bird – you know you are!
Fly close to the Scroobious Pip and say,
"Explain all about yourself we pray! –
For as yet we have neither seen nor heard
If you're Fish or Insect, Beast or Bird!"'

The Scroobious Pip looked gaily round
And sang these words with a chirpy sound –
    'Flippetty chip – Chippetty flip –
    My only name is the Scroobious Pip.'

The Scroobious Pip went into the sea
By the beautiful shore of the Jellybolee –
All the Fish in the world swam round
With a splashy squashy spluttery sound,
The Sprat, the Herring, the Turbot too,
The Shark, the Sole, and the Mackerel blue,
The ——————— spluttered, the Porpoise puffed
———Flounder ————————————————

And when the Whale began to spout –
———————————————————

And every Fish he shook the tip
Of his tail as he gazed on the Scroobious Pip.

At last they said to the Whale – 'By far
You're the biggest Fish – you know you are!
Swim close to the Scroobious Pip and say,
"Tell us all about yourself we pray! –   60
For to know from yourself is our only wish –
Are you Beast or Insect, Bird or Fish?"'

The Scroobious Pip looked softly round
And sang these words with a liquid sound -
        'Plifatty flip – Pliffity flip –
        My only name is the Scroobious Pip.'

The Scroobious Pip sate under a tree
By the silent shores of the Jellybolēē,
All the Insects in all the world
About the Scroobious Pip fluttered and twirled.   70
Beetles and ——— with purple eyes
Gnats and buzztilential Flies –
Grasshoppers, Butterflies, Spiders too,
Wasps and Bees and Dragonfly blue,
And when the Gnats began to hum
——— bounced like a dismal drum –
And every insect curled the tip
Of his snout, and looked at the Scroobious Pip.

At last they said the Ant, – 'By far
You're the wisest Insect – you know you are!   80
Creep close to the Scroobious Pip and say,
"Tell us all about yourself we pray! –
For we can't find out, and we can't tell why –
If you're Beast or Fish or a Bird or a Fly. –"'

The Scroobious Pip turned quickly round
And sang these words with a whistly sound –
   'Wizziby wip – wizziby wip –
   My only name is the Scroobious Pip.'

90   Then all the Beasts that walk on the ground
Danced in a circle round and round,
And all the Birds that fly in the air
Flew round and round in a circle there,
And all the Fish in the Jellybolee
Swam in a circle about the sea,
And all the Insects that creep or go
Buzzed in a circle to and fro –
And they roared and sang and whistled and cried
Till the noise was heard from side to side –
100   'Chippetty Tip! Chippetty Tip!
    Its only name is the Scroobious Pip.'

The Quangle Wangle's Hat

On the top of the Crumpetty Tree
   The Quangle Wangle sat,
But his face you could not see,
   On account of his Beaver Hat.
For his Hat was a hundred and two feet wide,
With ribbons and bibbons on every side,
And bells, and buttons, and loops, and lace,
So that nobody ever could see the face
      Of the Quangle Wangle Quee.

The Quangle Wangle said
   To himself on the Crumpetty Tree, –
'Jam; and jelly; and bread;
   Are the best of food for me!
But the longer I live on this Crumpetty Tree,
The plainer than ever it seems to me
That very few people come this way
And that life on the whole is far from gay!'
      Said the Quangle Wangle Quee.

But there came to the Crumpetty Tree,
   Mr and Mrs Canary;
And they said, – 'Did ever you see

10

20

Any spot so charmingly airy?
May we build a nest on your lovely Hat?
Mr Quangle Wangle, grant us that!
O please let us come and build a nest
Of whatever material suits you best,
        Mr Quangle Wangle Quee!'

And besides, to the Crumpetty Tree
    Came the Stork, the Duck, and the Owl;
The Snail, and the Bumble-Bee,
    The Frog, and the Fimble Fowl;
(The Fimble Fowl, with a Corkscrew leg;)
And all of them said, – 'We humbly beg,
We may build our homes on your lovely Hat, –
Mr Quangle Wangle, grant us that!
        Mr Quangle Wangle Quee!'

And the Golden Grouse came there,
    And the Pobble who has no toes, –
And the small Olympian bear, –
    And the Dong with a luminous nose.
And the Blue Baboon, who played the flute, –
And the Orient Calf from the Land of Tute, –
And the Attery Squash, and the Bisky Bat, –
All came and built on the lovely Hat
        Of the Quangle Wangle Quee.

And the Quangle Wangle said
    To himself on the Crumpetty Tree, –
'When all these creatures move
    What a wonderful noise there'll be!'
And at night by the light of the Mulberry moon
They danced to the Flute of the Blue Baboon,
On the broad green leaves of the Crumpetty Tree,
And all were as happy as happy could be,
        With the Quangle Wangle Quee.

[Receipt for George Scrivens, Esq.]

[Received August 2 1872   From George Scrivens Esqre.   The sum of
Ten Pounds, for a drawing of the Seeders of Lebanon.   Edward Lear.]

'Papa once went to Greece'

Papa once went to Greece,
And there I understand
He saw no end of lovely spots
About that lovely land.
He talks about these spots of Greece
To both Mama and me
Yet spots of Greece upon my dress
He can't abear to see!
I cannot make it out at all –
If ever on my frock
They see the smallest spot of Greece
It gives them quite a shock!
Henceforth, therefore, – to please them both
These spots of Greece no more
Shall be upon my frock at all –
Nor on my Pinafore.

The Story of the Pobble, who has no toes, and the Princess Bink

The Pobble who has no toes,
    Had once as many as we; –
When they said – 'Some day you may lose them all!' –
    He replied – 'Phum, phiddle de dee!' –
And his Aunt Jobiska made him drink
Lavender-water, tinged with pink,
For she said, – 'The world in general knows
There's nothing so good for a Pobble's toes!'

The Pobble who has no toes
    Swam across the Bristol Channel,
But before he went he swaddled his nose
    In a piece of scarlet flannel,

For his Aunt Jobiska said, – 'No harm
Can come to his toes if his nose is warm;
And it's perfectly known that a Pobble's toes
Are safe – provided he minds his nose!'

The Pobble swam fast and well,
    And when boats or ships came near him,
He tinkelty-binkelty-winkl'd a bell,
    So that all the world could hear him.   20
And all the Sailors and Admirals cried
When they saw him land on the farther side, –
'He has gone to fish for his Aunt Jobiska's
Runcible cat with crimson whiskers!'

The Pobble went gaily on,
    To a rock on the edge of the water,
And there, – a-eating of crumbs and cream,
    Sat King Jampoodle's daughter.
Her cap was a root of Beetroot red,
With a hole cut out to insert her head;   30
Her gloves were yellow; her shoes were pink,
Her frock was green; and her name was Bink.

Said the Pobble, – 'Oh Princess Bink,
    A-eating of crumbs and cream!
Your beautiful face has filled my heart
    With the most profound esteem!
And my Aunt Jobiska says, Man's life
Ain't worth a penny without a wife,
Whereby it will give me the greatest pleasure
If you'll marry me now, or when you've leisure!'   40

Said the Princess Bink – 'O! Yes!
    I will certainly cross the Channel
And marry you then if you'll give me now
    That lovely scarlet flannel!
And besides that flannel about your nose
I trust you will give me all your toes,

To place in my Pa's Museum collection,
As proof of your deep genteel affection.'

The Pobble unwrapped his nose,
    And gave her the flannel so red,
Which, throwing her Beetroot cap away, –
    She wreathed around her head.
And one by one he unscrewed his toes
Which were made of the beautiful wood that grows
In his Aunt Jobiska's roorial park,
When the days are short and the nights are dark.

Said the Princess – 'O Pobble! my Pobble!
    I'm yours for ever and ever!
I never will leave you my Pobble! my Pobble!
    Never, and never, and never!'
Said the Pobble – 'My Binky! O bless your heart! –
But say – would you like at once to start
Without taking leave of your dumpetty Father?
Jampoodle the King?' – Said the Princess – 'Rather!'

They crossed the Channel at once
    And when boats and ships came near them
They winkelty-binkelty-tinkled their bell
    So that all the world could hear them.
And all the Sailors and Admirals cried
When they saw them swim to the farther side, –
'There are no more fish for his Aunt Jobiska's
Runcible Cat with crimson whiskers!'

They danced about all day,
    All over the hills and dales;
They danced in every village and town
    In the North and the South of Wales.
And their Aunt Jobiska made them a dish
Of Mice and Buttercups fried with fish
For she said, – 'The World in general knows,
Pobbles are happier without their toes!'

The Pobble who has no Toes

The Pobble who has no toes
   Had once as many as we;
When they said, 'Some day you may lose them all;' –
   He replied, –'Fish fiddle de-dee!'
And his Aunt Jobiska made him drink,
Lavender water tinged with pink,
For she said, 'The World in general knows
There's nothing so good for a Pobble's toes!'

The Pobble who has no toes,
   Swam across the Bristol Channel;   10
But before he set out he wrapped his nose,
   In a piece of scarlet flannel.
For his Aunt Jobiska said, 'No harm
Can come to his toes if his nose is warm;
And it's perfectly known that a Pobble's toes
Are safe, – provided he minds his nose.'

The Pobble swam fast and well,
   And when boats or ships came near him
He tinkledy-binkledy-winkled a bell,
   So that all the world could hear him.   20

And all the Sailors and Admirals cried,
When they saw him nearing the further side, –
'He has gone to fish for his Aunt Jobiska's
Runcible Cat with crimson whiskers!'

But before he touched the shore,
    The shore of the Bristol Channel,
A sea-green Porpoise carried away
    His wrapper of scarlet flannel.
And when he came to observe his feet,
Formerly garnished with toes so neat,
His face at once became forlorn
On perceiving that all his toes were gone!

And nobody ever knew
    From that dark day to the present,
Whoso had taken the Pobble's toes,
    In a manner so far from pleasant.
Whether the shrimps or crawfish gray,
Or crafty Mermaids stole them away –
Nobody knew; and nobody knows
How the Pobble was robbed of his twice five toes!

The Pobble who has no toes
    Was placed in a friendly Bark,
And they rowed him back, and carried him up,
    To his Aunt Jobiska's Park.
And she made him a feast at his earnest wish
Of eggs and buttercups fried with fish; –
And she said, – 'It's a fact the whole world knows,
That Pobbles are happier without their toes.'

The Akond of Swat

Who, or why, or which, or *what*, Is the Akond of SWAT?

Is he tall or short, or dark or fair?
Does he sit on a stool or a sofa or chair   or SQUAT,
                                        The Akond of Swat?

Is he wise or foolish, young or old?
Does he drink his soup and his coffee cold   or HOT,
                                        The Akond of Swat?

Does he sing or whistle, jabber or talk,
And when riding abroad does he gallop or walk   or TROT,
                                        The Akond of Swat?   10

Does he wear a turban, a fez, or a hat?
Does he sleep on a mattress, a bed, or a mat   or a COT,
                                        The Akond of Swat?

When he writes a copy in round-hand size,
Does he cross his T's and finish his I's   with a DOT,
                                        The Akond of Swat?

Can he write a letter concisely clear
Without a speck or a smudge or a smear   or BLOT,
                                        The Akond of Swat?

Do his people like him extremely well?   20
Or do they, whenever they can, rebel   or PLOT,
                                        At the Akond of Swat?

If he catches them then, either old or young,
Does he have them chopped in pieces or hung   or SHOT,
                                        The Akond of Swat?

Do his people prig in the lanes or park?
Or even at times, when days are dark   GAROTTE,
                                        O the Akond of Swat!

Does he study the wants of his own dominion?
Or doesn't he care for public opinion   a JOT,   30
                                        The Akond of Swat?

To amuse his mind do his people show him
Pictures, or anyone's last new poem   or WHAT,
                                        For the Akond of Swat?

At night if he suddenly screams and wakes,
Do they bring him only a few small cakes   or a LOT,
                                        For the Akond of Swat?

Does he live on turnips, tea, or tripe?
Does he like his shawl to be marked with a stripe   or a DOT,
                                        The Akond of Swat?

Does he like to lie on his back in a boat
Like the lady who lived in that isle remote,   SHALOTT,
                                        The Akond of Swat?

Is he quiet, or always making a fuss?
Is his steward a Swiss or a Swede or a Russ   or a SCOT,
                                        The Akond of Swat?

Does he like to sit by the calm blue wave?
Or to sleep and snore in a dark green cave   or a GROTT,
                                        The Akond of Swat?

Does he drink small beer from a silver jug?
Or a bowl? or a glass? or a cup? or a mug?   or a POT,
                                        The Akond of Swat?

Does he beat his wife with a gold-topped pipe,
When she lets the gooseberries grow too ripe   or ROT,
                                        The Akond of Swat?

Does he wear a white tie when he dines with friends,
And tie it neat in a bow with ends   or a KNOT,
                                        The Akond of Swat?

Does he like new cream, and hate mince-pies?
When he looks at the sun does he wink his eyes   or NOT,
                                        The Akond of Swat?

Does he teach his subjects to roast and bake?
Does he sail about on an inland lake   in a YACHT,
                                        The Akond of Swat?

Someone, or nobody, knows I wot
Who or which or why or what   Is the Akond of Swat!

The Akond
of Swat

'The Attalik Ghaz*ee*'

The Attalik Ghaz*ee*
Had a wife whose name was Jee
And a Lady proud was she,
While residing by the sea.

Said the Attalik Ghaz*ee*
(Who resided by the sea,)
'My own beloved Jee!
I am suffering from a flea
Which has settled on my knee.'

Said the Begum Lady Jee
(Who resided by the sea,)
'Why! What is that to me?
Do you think I'll catch a flea
That has settled on your knee?'

[Indian limericks]

There was an old man of Narkūnder,
Whose voice was like peals of loud thunder;
It shivered the hills into Colocynth Pills,
And destroyed half the trees of Narkūnder.

There lived a small puppy at Nārkunda,
Who sought for the best tree to bārk under;
Which he found, and said, 'Now, I can call out Bow wow
Underneath the best Cedar in Nārkundar.'

There was a small child at Narkūnda,
Who said, 'Don't you hear! That is thunder!'
But they said, 'It's the Bonzes, a-making responses,
In a temple eight miles from Narkūnda.'

There was an old man of Teōg,
Who purchased that Nārkunder dog,
Whom he fed on the hills, with those Colocynth pills,
Till he wholly ran off from Teōg.

There was an old man of Mahasso,
Who sang both as Tenor and Basso;
His voice was that high, it went into the sky,
And came down again quite to Mahasso.

There was an old person of Fágoo,
Who purchased a ship and its Cargo;
    When the Sails were all furled,
    He sailed all round the world,
And returned all promiscuous to Fágoo.

There was an old man in a Tonga,
Who said, 'If this ride lasts much longer, –
    Between shaking and dust,
    I shall probably bust,
And never ride more in a Tonga.'

'O! Chichester, my Carlingford!'

O! Chichester, my Carlingford!
O! Parkinson, my Sam!
O! SPQ, my Fortescue!
How awful glad I am!

For now you'll do no more hard work
Because by sudden=pleasing jerk
You're all at once a peer, –
Whereby I cry, 'God bless the Queen!
As was, and is, and still has been.'
Yours ever, Edward Lear.

The Cummerbund

An Indian Poem

She sate upon her Dobie,
    To watch the Evening Star,
And all the Punkahs as they passed,
    Cried, 'My! how fair you are!'
Around her bower, with quivering leaves,
    The tall Kamsamahs grew,
And Kitmutgars in wild festoons
    Hung down from Tchokis blue.

Below her home the river rolled
    With soft meloobious sound,   10
Where golden-finned Chuprassies swam,
    In myriads circling round.
Above, on tallest trees remote,
    Green Ayahs perched alone,
And all night long the Mussak moan'd
    Its melancholy tone.

And where the purple Nullahs threw
    Their branches far and wide, –
The silvery Goreewallahs flew
    In silence, side by side, –   20
The little Bheesties' twittering cry
    Rose on the flagrant air,
And oft the angry Jampan howled
    Deep in his hateful lair.

She sate upon her Dobie, –
    She heard the Nimmak hum, –
When all at once a cry arose, –
    'The Cummerbund is come!'
In vain she fled: – with open jaws
    The angry monster followed,   30

And so, (before assistance came,)
    That Lady Fair was swollowed.

They sought in vain for even a bone
    Respectfully to bury, –
They said, – 'Hers was a dreadful fate!'
    (And Echo answered 'Very.')
They nailed her Dobie to the wall,
    Where last her form was seen,
And underneath they wrote these words,
    In yellow, blue, and green: –

'Beware, ye Fair! Ye Fair, beware!
    Nor sit out late at night, –
Lest horrid Cummerbunds should come,
    And swollow you outright.'

Letter to Lady Wyatt

Dear Lady Wyatt,

If I a*m inte*rrupting you please excuse me
as I *mint* to have asked you a question the other day
but forgot to *mint*=ion it. Can you tell me how to make
preserved or dry *mint*? I have got a
mint of
mint in my garden, but although I
a*m int*=erested in getting some of it dried for
pea-soup, I a*m in t*errible ignorance of how to dry it,
and a*m in t*orture till I know how. On cutting the
leaves, should they be *mint*'sd up small like   10
mint'sd meat? – or should I put
the*m into* Gin & Tarragon vinegar? Or place them
in a jar of *Mint*on pottery, & expose them to the
ele*mint*s in a
her*mint*ically sealed bottle? If Mr Disraeli,
who is now Prime *mint*=stir, could teach us how to stir
the *mint*,
I a*m int*ernally convinced we could manage it.
This is as plain as that the *Mint*cio is a large River in Italy, or that
Lord *Mint*o was once Governor Genl. of India. Perhaps   20
at the rising of Palia*mint*, he may help us. After all would the
success be com*mint*surate with the trouble?
What com*mint* can be made on this except
that Mrs Wyatt should send To*m into* the country if he is unwell in town?
One thing is sure, all ver*mint* must be carefully excluded
from the bottle, & I a*m inte*nding to get one really well
made, for I a*m int*oxicated with the idea of getting good dry
mint. Please if you have a receipt, give it me
which will be a monu*mint* of your good nature.
*Mint*ime I   30
a*m in t*oo much haste to write any
more, so will leave off im*mint*iately.

Yours sincerely,
Edward Lear

Poona Observer, May 1875.

We are able to present our readers with an inaccurate misrepresentation of the well known Author & Artist Mr Edward Lear, who has lately caused so much sensation in our city by having become a Fakeer. He may be seen any day beneath the 18th Banyan tree on the wrong hand as you descend the level road entering and leaving Poonah from Peshawar and Madras. He is constantly attended by a tame crow & a large dog of the Grumpsifactious species, & passes his days in placid conkimplation of the surrounding scenery. –

The New Vestments

There lived an old man in the Kingdom of Tess,
Who invented a purely original dress;
And when it was perfectly made and complete,
He opened the door, and walked into the street.

By way of a hat, he'd a loaf of Brown Bread,
In the middle of which he inserted his head; –
His Shirt was made up of no end of dead Mice,
The warmth of whose skins was quite fluffy and nice; –
His Drawers were of Rabbit-skins; – so were his Shoes; –
His Stockings were skins, – but it is not known whose; –   10
His Waistcoat and Trowsers were made of Pork Chops; –
His Buttons were Jujubes, and Chocolate Drops; –
His Coat was all Pancakes with Jam for a border,
And a girdle of Biscuits to keep it in order;
And he wore over all, as a screen from bad weather,
A Cloak of green Cabbage-leaves stitched all together.

He had walked a short way, when he heard a great noise,
Of all sorts of Beasticles, Birdlings, and Boys; –
And from every long street and dark lane in the town
Beasts, Birdles, and Boys in a tumult rushed down.   20
Two Cows and a Calf ate his Cabbage-leaf Cloak; –
Four Apes seized his Girdle, which vanished like smoke; –
Three Kids ate up half of his Pancaky Coat, –
And the tails were devour'd by an ancient He Goat; –
An army of Dogs in a twinkling tore *up* his
Pork Waistcoat and Trowsers to give to their Puppies; –
And while they were growling, and mumbling the Chops,
Ten Boys prigged the Jujubes and Chocolate Drops. –
He tried to run back to his house, but in vain,
For Scores of fat Pigs came again and again; –   30
They rushed out of stables and hovels and doors, –
They tore off his stockings, his shoes, and his drawers; –

And now from the housetops with screechings descend,
Striped, spotted, white, black, and gray Cats without end,
They jumped on his shoulders and knocked off his hat, –
When Crows, Ducks, and Hens made a mincemeat of that; –
They speedily flew at this sleeves in a trice,
And utterly tore up his Shirt of dead Mice; –
They swallowed the last of his Shirt with a squall, –
40   Whereon he ran home with no clothes on at all.

And he said to himself as he bolted the door,
'I will not wear a similar dress any more,
Any more, any more, any more, never more!'

The Pelican Chorus

King and Queen of the Pelicans we;
No other Birds so grand we see!
None but we have feet like fins!
With lovely leathery throats and chins!
    Ploffskin, Pluffskin, Pelican jee!
    We think no Birds so happy as we!
    Plumpskin, Ploshkin, Pelican jill!
    We think so then, and we thought so still!

We live on the Nile. The Nile we love.
By night we sleep on the cliffs above;
By day we fish, and at eve we stand
On long bare islands of yellow sand.
And when the sun sinks slowly down
And the great rock walls grow dark and brown,
When the purple river rolls fast and dim
And the Ivory Ibis starlike skim,
Wing to wing we dance around, –
Stamping our feet with a flumpy sound, –
Opening our mouths as Pelicans ought,
And this is the song we nightly snort; –

> Ploffskin, Pluffskin, Pelican jee!
> We think no Birds so happy as we!
> Plumpskin, Ploshkin, Pelican jill!
> We think so then, and we thought so still!

Last year came out our Daughter, Dell;
And all the Birds received her well.
To do her honour, a feast we made
For every bird that can swim or wade.
Herons and Gulls, and Cormorants black,
Cranes, and Flamingos with scarlet back,   30
Plovers and Storks, and Geese in clouds,
Swans and Dilberry Ducks in crowds.
Thousands of Birds in wondrous flight!
They ate and drank and danced all night,
And echoing back from the rocks you heard
Multitude-echoes from Bird and Bird, –

> Ploffskin, Pluffskin, Pelican jee!
> We think no Birds so happy as we!
> Plumpskin, Ploshkin, Pelican jill!
> We think so then, and we thought so still!   40

Yes, they came; and among the rest,
The King of the Cranes all grandly dressed.
Such a lovely tail! Its feathers float
Between the ends of his blue dress-coat;
With pea-green trowsers all so neat,
And a delicate frill to hide his feet, –
(For though no one speaks of it, every one knows,
He has got no webs between his toes!)

As soon as he saw our Daughter Dell,
In violent love that Crane King fell, –   50
On seeing her waddling form so fair,
With a wreath of shrimps in her short white hair.
And before the end of the next long day,
Our Dell had given her heart away;

For the King of the Cranes had won that heart,
With a Crocodile's egg and a large fish-tart.
She vowed to marry the King of the Cranes,
Leaving the Nile for stranger plains;
And away they flew in a gathering crowd
60 Of endless birds in a lengthening cloud.
    Ploffskin, Pluffskin, Pelican jee!
    We think no Birds so happy as we!
    Plumpskin, Ploshkin, Pelican jill!
    We think so then, and we thought so still!

And far away in the twilight sky,
We heard them singing a lessening cry, –
Farther and farther till out of sight,
And we stood alone in the silent night!
Often since, in the nights of June,
70 We sit on the sand and watch the moon; –
She has gone to the great Gromboolian plain,
And we probably never shall meet again!
Oft, in the long still nights of June,
We sit on the rocks and watch the moon; –
– She dwells by the streams of the Chankly Bore,
And we probably never shall see her more.
    Ploffskin, Pluffskin, Pelican jee!
    We think no Birds so happy as we!
    Plumpskin, Ploshkin, Pelican jill!
80   We think so then, and we thought so still!

The Two Old Bachelors

Two old Bachelors were living in one house;
One caught a Muffin, the other caught a Mouse.
Said he who caught the Muffin to him who caught the Mouse, –
'This happens just in time! For we've nothing in the house,
Save a tiny slice of lemon and a teaspoonful of honey,
And what to do for dinner – since we haven't any money?
And what can we expect if we haven't any dinner,
But to lose our teeth and eyelashes and keep on growing thinner?'

Said he who caught the Mouse to him who caught the Muffin, –
'We might cook this little Mouse, if we only had some Stuffin'!   10
If we had but Sage and Onion we could do extremely well,
But how to get that Stuffin' it is difficult to tell!' –

Those two old Bachelors ran quickly to the town
And asked for Sage and Onions as they wandered up and down;
They borrowed two large Onions, but no Sage was to be found
In the Shops, or in the Market, or in all the Gardens round.

But someone said, – 'A hill there is, a little to the north,
And to its purpledicular top a narrow way leads forth; –
And there among the rugged rocks abides an ancient Sage, –
An earnest Man, who reads all day a most perplexing page.   20

Climb up, and seize him by the toes! – all studious as he sits, –
And pull him down, – and chop him into endless little bits!
Then mix him with your Onion, (cut up likewise into Scraps,) –
When your Stuffin' will be ready – and very good: perhaps.'

Those two old Bachelors without loss of time
The nearly purpledicular crags at once began to climb;
And at the top, among the rocks, all seated in a nook,
They saw that Sage, a-reading of a most enormous book.

'You earnest Sage!' aloud they cried, 'your book you've read
    enough in! –
We wish to chop you into bits to mix you into Stuffin'!' –

But that old Sage looked calmly up, and with his awful book,
At those two Bachelors' bald heads a certain aim he took; –
And over crag and precipice they rolled promiscuous down, –
At once they rolled, and never stopped in lane or field or town, –
And when they reached their house, they found (beside their want
    of Stuffin')
The Mouse had fled; – and, previously, had eaten up the Muffin.

They left their home in silence by the once convivial door.
And from that hour those Bachelors were never heard of more.

[Nonsense Botany – 3]

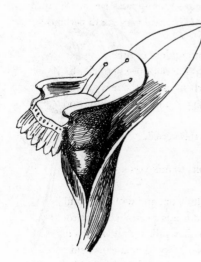

Armchairia Comfortabilis

Bassia Palealensis

Bubblia Blowpipia

Bluebottlia Buzztilentia

Crabbia Horrida

Smalltoothcombia Domestica

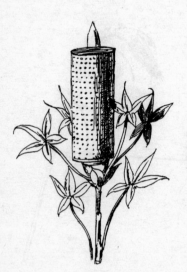

Knutmigrata Simplice

Tureenia Ladlecum

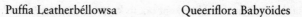

Puffia Leatherbéllowsa   Queeriflora Babyöides

'A tumbled down, and hurt his Arm, against a bit of wood'

A tumbled down, and hurt his Arm, against a bit of wood.

B said, 'My Boy, O! do not cry; it cannot do you good!'

C said, 'A Cup of Coffee hot can't do you any harm.'

D said, 'A Doctor should be fetched, and he would cure the arm.'

E said, 'An Egg beat up with milk would quickly make him well.'

F said, 'A Fish, if broiled, might cure, if only by the smell.'

G said, 'Green Gooseberry fool, the best of cures I hold.'

H said, 'His Hat should be kept on, to keep him from the cold.'

I said, 'Some Ice upon his head will make him better soon.'

J said, 'Some Jam, if spread on bread, or given in a spoon!'

K said, 'A Kangaroo is here, – this picture let him see.'

L said, 'A Lamp pray keep alight, to make some barley tea.'

M said, 'A Mulberry or two might give him satisfaction.'

N said, 'Some Nuts, if rolled about, might be a slight attraction.'

O said, 'An Owl might make him laugh, if only it would wink.'

P said, 'Some Poetry might be read aloud, to make him think.'

Q said, 'A Quince I recommend, – a Quince, or else a Quail.'

R said, 'Some Rats might make him move, if fastened by their tail.'

S said, 'A Song should now be sung, in hopes to make him laugh!'

T said, 'A Turnip might avail, if sliced or cut in half!'

U said, 'An Urn, with water hot, place underneath his chin!'

V said, 'I'll stand upon a chair, and play a Violin!'

W said, 'Some Whisky-Whizzgigs fetch, some marbles and a ball!'

X said, 'Some double XX ale would be the best of all!'

Y said, 'Some Yeast mixed up with salt would make a perfect plaster!'

Z said, 'Here is a box of Zinc! Get in, my little master!
    We'll shut you up! We'll nail you down! We will, my little master!
    We think we've all heard quite enough of this your sad disaster!'

The Dong with a Luminous Nose

When awful darkness and silence reign
　　Over the great Gromboolian plain,
　　　　Through the long, long wintry nights; –
When the angry breakers roar
As they beat on the rocky shore; –
　　　　When Storm-clouds brood on the towering heights
Of the Hills of the Chankly Bore: –

Then, through the vast and gloomy dark,
There moves what seems a fiery spark,
　　　　A lonely spark with silvery rays
　　　　Piercing the coal-black night, –
　　　　A Meteor strange and bright: –
Hither and thither the vision strays,
　　　　A single lurid light.

Slowly it wanders, – pauses, – creeps, –
Anon it sparkles, – flashes and leaps;
And ever as onward it gleaming goes
A light on the Bong-tree stems it throws.
And those who watch at that midnight hour
From Hall or Terrace, or lofty Tower,

Cry, as the wild light passes along, –
    'The Dong! – the Dong!
    The wandering Dong through the forest goes!
        The Dong! the Dong!
    The Dong with a luminous Nose!'

        Long years ago
        The Dong was happy and gay,
Till he fell in love with a Jumbly Girl
    Who came to those shores one day.
For the Jumblies came in a sieve, they did, –   30
Landing at eve near the Zemmery Fidd
        Where the Oblong Oysters grow,
        And the rocks are smooth and gray.
And all the woods and the valleys rang
With the Chorus they daily and nightly sang, –
        Far and few, far and few,
        Are the lands where the Jumblies live;
        Their heads are green, and their hands are blue,
        And they went to sea in a sieve.'

Happily, happily passed those days!   40
        While the cheerful Jumblies staid;
        They danced in circlets all night long,
        To the plaintive pipe of the lively Dong,
            In moonlight, shine, or shade.
For day and night he was always there
By the side of the Jumbly Girl so fair,
With her sky-blue hands, and her sea-green hair.
Till the morning came of that hateful day
When the Jumblies sailed in their sieve away,
And the Dong was left on the cruel shore   50
Gazing – gazing for evermore, –
Ever keeping his weary eyes on
That pea-green sail on the far horizon, –
Singing the Jumbly Chorus still
As he sate all day on the grassy hill, –

'Far and few, far and few,
Are the lands where the Jumblies live;
Their heads are green, and their hands are blue,
And they went to sea in a sieve.'

60   But when the sun was low in the West,
The Dong arose and said; –
– 'What little sense I once possessed
Has quite gone out of my head!' –
And since that day he wanders still
By lake and forest, marsh and hill,
Singing – 'O somewhere, in valley or plain
Might I find my Jumbly Girl again!
For ever I'll seek by lake and shore
Till I find my Jumbly Girl once more!'

70   Playing a pipe with silvery squeaks,
Since then his Jumbly Girl he seeks,
And because by night he could not see,
He gathered the bark of the Twangum Tree
On the flowery plain that grows.
And he wove him a wondrous Nose, –
A Nose as strange as a Nose could be!
Of vast proportions and painted red,
And tied with cords to the back of his head.
– In a hollow rounded space it ended
80   With a luminous Lamp within suspended,
All fenced about
With a bandage stout
To prevent the wind from blowing it out; –
And with holes all round to send the light,
In gleaming rays on the dismal light.

And now each night, and all night long,
Over those plains still roams the Dong;
And above the wail of the Chimp and Snipe
You may hear the squeak of his plaintive pipe

While ever he seeks, but seeks in vain   90
To meet with his Jumbly Girl again;
Lonely and wild – all night he goes, –
The Dong with a luminous Nose!
And all who watch at the midnight hour,
From Hall or Terrace, or lofty Tower,
Cry, as they trace the Meteor bright,
Moving along through the dreary night, –
      'This is the hour when forth he goes,
      The Dong with a luminous Nose!
      Yonder – over the plain he goes;   100
          He goes!
          He goes;
      The Dong with a luminous Nose!'

'Finale Marina! If ever you'd seen her!'

Finale Marina! If ever you'd seen her!
Your heart had been quickly enslaved.
Her eyes were pea-green, and her bonnet was greener,
And wonderful fine she behaved!

In medio Tutorissimus ibis
'Thou shalt walk in the midst of thy Tutors'

Once on a time a youthful cove
    As was a cheery lad
Lived in a Willa by the sea. –
    The cove was not so bad;

The dogs and cats, the cow and ass,
    The birds in cage or grove,
The rabbits, hens, ducks, pony – pigs
    All loved that cheery cove.

Some folk, – one female and six male, –
    Seized on that youthful cove;
They said, – 'To edjukate this chap
    Us seven it doth behove.'

The first his parient was, – who taught
    The cove to read and ride,
Latin, and Grammarithmetic,
    And lots of things beside.

Says Pa, 'I'll spare no pains or time
    Your school hours so to cut,
And square and fit, that you will make
    No end of progress – *but* –'

Says Mrs Grey, – 'I'll teach him French,
    Pour parler dans cette pays, –
Je crois qui'il parlerà bien;
    Même comme un Français – *mais*, –'

Says Signor Gambinossi, – 'Si;
    Progresso si farà,
Lo voglio insegnare qui,
    La Lingua mia – *ma* –'

Says Mr Crump, – 'Geology,
    And Matthewmatics stiff,
I'll teach the cove, who's sure to go
    Ahead like blazes, – *if* –'

Says James, – 'I'll teach him every day
    My Nastics; – now and then
To stand upon his 'ed; and make
    His mussels harder, – *when* –'

Says Signor Blanchi, ' – Lascia far; –
    La musica da me,
Ben insegnata gli sarà; –
    Farà progresso, – *se* –'   40

Says Edward Lear, – 'I'll make him draw
    A Palace, or a hut,
Trees, mountains, rivers, cities, plains,
    And prapps to paint them, – *but* – '

So all these seven joined hands and sang
    This chorus by the sea; –
'O! Ven his edjukation's done,
    Vy! Vot a cove he'll be!'

'O dear! how disgusting is life!'

O dear! how disgusting is life!
To improve it O what can we do?
Most disgusting is hustle and strife,
And of all things an ill fitting shoe –
    Shoe
        O bother an ill fitting shoe!

'How pleasant to know Mr Lear!'

From a Photograph.

'How pleasant to know Mr Lear!'
  Who has written such volumes of stuff!
Some think him ill-tempered and queer,
  But a few think him pleasant enough.

His mind is concrete and fastidious; –
  His nose is remarkably big; –
His visage is more or less hideous; –
  His beard it resembles a wig.

He has ears, and two eyes, and ten fingers, –
  (Leastways if you reckon two thumbs;)
Long ago he was one of the singers,
  But now he is one of the dumms.

He sits in a beautiful parlour,
  With hundreds of books on the wall;
He drinks a great deal of Marsala,
  But never gets tipsy at all.

He has many friends, laymen and clerical;
    Old Foss is the name of his cat;
His body is perfectly spherical; –
    He weareth a runcible hat.   20

When he walks in a waterproof white
    The children run after him *so*!
Calling out, – 'He's come out in his night-
    gown, that crazy old Englishman, – O!'

He weeps by the side of the ocean,
    He weeps on the top of the hill;
He purchases pancakes and lotion,
    And chocolate shrimps from the mill.

He reads, but he cannot speak, Spanish;
    He cannot abide ginger-beer. –   30
Ere the days of his pilgrimage vanish, –
    'How pleasant to know Mr Lear!'

Mr and Mrs Discobbolos
Second Part

Mr and Mrs Discobbolos
    Lived on the top of the wall,
  For twenty years, a month and a day,
  Till their hair had grown all pearly gray,
    And their teeth began to fall.
They never were ill, or at all dejected, –
By all admired, and by some respected,
    Till Mrs Discobbolos said,
    'O W! X! Y! Z!
    It is just come into my head –
  We have no more room at all –
        Darling Mr Discobbolos!

'Look at our six fine boys!
    And our six sweet girls so fair!
  Up on this wall they have all been born,
  And not one of the twelve has happened to fall,
    Through my maternal care!
Surely they should not pass their lives
Without any chance of husbands or wives!'
    And Mrs Discobbolos said,
    'O W! X! Y! Z!
    Did it never come into your head
  That our lives must be lived elsewhere,
        Dearest Mr Discobbolos?

'They have never been at a Ball,
    Nor have even seen a Bazaar!
  Nor have heard folks say in a tone all hearty, –
  "What loves of girls (at a garden party)
    Those Misses Discobbolos are!"
Morning and night it drives me wild
To think of the fate of each darling child, – ! –'
    But Mr Discobbolos said,

'O – W! X! Y! Z!
What has come into your fiddledum head!
What a runcible goose you are!
            Octopod Mrs Discobbolos!'

Suddenly Mr Discobbolos
        Slid from the top of the wall;
    And beneath it he dug a dreadful trench, –
    And filled it with Dynamite gunpowder gench, –   40
        And aloud began to call, –
'Let the wild bee sing and the blue bird hum!
For the end of our lives has certainly come!'
        And Mrs Discobbolos said,
        'O! W! X! Y! Z!
    We shall presently all be dead,
    On this ancient runcible wall, –
            Terrible Mr Discobbolos!'

Pensively, Mr Discobbolos
        Sate with his back to the wall; –   50
    He lighted a match, and fired the train, –
        And the mortified mountains echoed again
        To the sounds of an awful fall!
And all the Discobbolos family flew
 In thousands of bits to the sky so blue,
        And no one was left to have said,
        'O! W! X! Y! Z!
    Has it come into anyone's head
    That the end has happened to all
            Of the whole of the Clan Discobbolos?'   60

'O Brother Chicken! Sister Chick!'

O Brother Chicken! Sister Chick!
  O gracious me! O my!
This broken Eggshell was my home!
  I see it with my eye!
However did I get inside? Or how did I get out?
And must my life be evermore, an atmosphere of doubt?

Can no one tell? Can no one solve, this mystery of Eggs?
Or why we chirp and flap our wings, – or why we've all two legs?
And since we cannot understand, –
    May it not seem to me,
That we were merely born by chance,
    Egg-nostics for to be?

'Dear Sir, Though many checks prevent'

Dear Sir, Though many checks prevent
More tours in Isle or Continent,
(Checks once I minded not a pin, –
Advancing years, or want of tin, –)
Yet of all checks the best is found,
A Cheque for Five and Thirty Pound.

So for such cheque upon your *Bank, you*
Sent me just now, I beg to *thank you*;
(Besides your letter – and for *this 'tis in*
εγὼ προσφέρω *εὐχαρίστησιν.–*
And so I sign me – your sincere
Obliged admirer, *Edward Lear.*

(As for the Picture, that will *quick and soon*
Be sent to Messrs Foord and *Dickenson.*)

Remminissenciz of Orgust 14 Aitnundrednaity

There was a great Person of Stratton,
Who fell fast asleep with his Hat=on.
     He slept for one hour,
     And awoke with more power
To leave Micheldéver for Stratton.

'I am awfull aged in apierance lately
and am exactly like this.'

There was an old man with a ribbon,
Who found a large volume of Gibbon,
Which he tied to his nose –
And said – 'I suppose
This is quite the best use for my ribbon.'

Letter to Mrs Stuart Wortley [The Moon Journey]

My dear Mrs Stuart Wortley,

In the first place observe the Envellope, for the appearance of which an oppology is kneaded, the fact being that there was only this one in the house large enough, & so, though it was originally addressed to the Hon. J. Warren, I altered it to what it now is. Secondly, I thought it so kind of you to have purchased the Mte Generoso drawing, that I wanted you to have 2 scraps to remind you of 'Simla', and 'Ravenna forest'. Which two I enclose, hoping you may think them worth a corner in some Album. I also send 2 still smaller, – one for each of the young Ladies.

These are of singular – I may say bingular value, – as they were done in the Moon, to which I lately went one night, returning next morning on a Moonbeam. As the Signorine Blanche & Katherine appreciate nonsense, I will add some few notes concerning the 2 subjects which I got with great rapidity during my visit, nothing being easier in that wonderful country than to travel thousands of miles in a minute. And these journeys are all done by means of Moonbeams, which, far from being mere portions of light, are in reality living creatures, endowed with considerable sogassity, & a long nose like the truck of a Nelliphant, though this is quite imperceptible to the naked eye. You have only to whisper to the Moonbeam what you wish to see, & you are there in a moment, & its nose or trunk being placed round your body, you cannot by any possibility fall.

The first view it is of the Jizzdoddle rocks, with 2 of the many remarkable planets which surround the moon rising or riz in the distance; these orange-coloured & peagreen orbs leaving a profound impression of sensational surprise on the mind of the speckletator who first beholds them. The second view represents the Rumbytumby ravine, with the crimson planet Buzz and its 5 Satanites on the horizon. In the foreground on the left is a Blompopp tree, so called from the Blompopp, a gigantic and gorgeous bird which builds on its summit. To the left are the tall Vizzikilly trees, the most common vegetation of the Lunar hummysphere. These trees grow to an immense height, & bloom only once in 15 years, when they produce a large crop of immemorial soapbubbles, submarine sucking-pigs, songs of sunrise, & silver sixpences, – which last are ground into powder by the Lunar population, & drunk in warm water without any sugar.

So little is known of the inhabitants of the moon, that a few descriptive but accurate notices relating to them may be interesting. They do not in the least resemble the people of our world, – as for instance they are all much broader than they are high; they have no hair on their heads, – but on the contrary a beautiful crest of yellow feathers which they can raise or depress at will, like that of the ordinary Cockatoo. And from the tip of their nose depends an elegant and affecting bunch of hair, sometimes extending to as much as 20 miles in length, and as it is considered sacrilegious to cut it, it is gradually wound round a silvergilt post firmly placed in the ground, but removable at pleasure. The faces of the more educated classes have a pensively perverse and placid expression, – not unlike the countenance of an Oyster, while frequently a delicately doubleminded semi-visual obliquity adds a pathos to their pungent physiognomy.

These remarkable people, so unlike ourselves, pass 18 months of their year (which consists of 22) in the strictest seclusion, – suspended with their heads downwards, and held carefully in crimson silk bags, – which are severely & suddenly shaken from time to time by select servants. Thus, – exempt from the futile & fluctuating fatuity of fashion, these estimable creatures pass an indigenous life of indefinite duration surrounded by their admiring ancestors, & despised by their incipient posterity. Their servants are not natives of the Moon, but are brought at great expense from a negative although nutritious star at a remote distance, and are wholly of a different species from the Lunar population, having 8 arms & 8 legs each, but no head whatever; – only a chin in the middle of which are their eyes, – their mouths, (of which each individual possesses 8,) being one in each little toe, & with these they discourse with an overpowering volubility & an indiscriminating alacrity surprising to contemplate. The conduct of these singular domestics is usually virtuous & voluminous, & their general aspic highly mucilaginous & meritorious.

I have no time at present to dilate further on other particulars of Lunar Natural History; – the prevalence of 2 sorts of gales, gales of wind and nightingales; – the general inebriety of the Atmosphere; – or the devotional functions of the inhabitants, consisting chiefly in the immense consumption of Ambleboff pies.

Hoping that I may see you & the 2 two young ladies on Wednesday,
    Believe me,
        Yours sincerely,
            Edward Lear.

[Chichester Fortescue is appointed Lord Privy Seal]

A curious circumstance and one worthy of note must also be recorded, because a similar fact is not found in the ceremonies of any other Royal Court whatsoever.

Before the guests go to their rooms, – after the Queen has left the Gallery, – the President of the Privy Council is seen entering, followed by 10 servants in livery, not however as President, but as Guardian of the Great Seal, – a post of the greatest importance and significance, and only given to the most trustworthy, learned, clever, and amiable gentlemen of the Court.

By the side of the Lord Guardian, and held by him by means of a chain, the Seal – which has no feet – makes its progress all through the Gallery, and is so to speak, taken to make the acquaintance of all the guests. One cannot well describe the motion of this enormous animal, as Italian is lacking in words that adequately translate 'Wallop' or 'Flump', verbs that well suit its motion, but that are unknown to us Italians. Many ladies are a good deal frightened the first time that they see the Great Seal, but they are strictly forbidden to scream. When it has been all round the Gallery, this amiable beast withdraws again with a Wallop-flump, with the Lord Guardian; – and before retiring, the latter gives the Seal more that 37 pounds of macaroni, 18 bottles of Champagne, 2 beefsteaks, and a ball of scarlet worsted – all of which are brought by 10 servants in livery.

[Nonsense Trees]

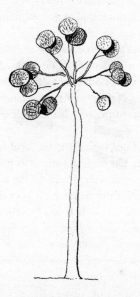

The Biscuit Tree

This remarkable vegetable production has never yet been described or delineated. As it never grows near rivers, nor near the sea, nor near mountains, or vallies, or houses, – its native place is wholly uncertain. When the flowers fall off, and the tree breaks out in biscuits, the effect is by no means disagreeable, especially to the hungry. – If the Biscuits grow in pairs, they do not grow single, and if they ever fall off, they cannot be said to remain on. –

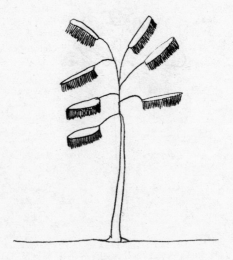

The Clothes-Brush Tree

This most useful natural production does not produce many clothes-brushes, which accounts for those objects being expensive. The omsquombious nature of this extraordinary vegetable it is of course unnecessary to be diffuse upon.

The Fork Tree

This pleasing and amazing Tree never grows above four hundred and sixty-three feet in height, – nor has any specimen hitherto produced above forty thousand silver forks at one time. If violently shaken it is most probable that many forks would fall off, – and in a high wind it is highly possible that all the forks would rattle dreadfully, and produce a musical tinkling to the ears of the happy beholder.

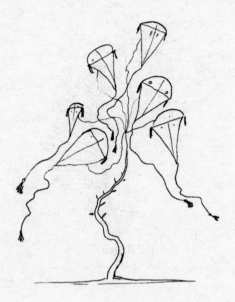

The Kite Tree

The Kite Tree is a fearful and astonishing vegetable when all the Kites are agitated by a tremendous wind, and endeavour to escape from their strings. The tree does not appear to be of any particular use to society, but would be frequented by small boys if they knew where it grew.

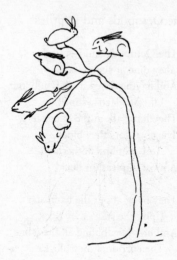

The Rabbit Tree

The Clomjombimbilious Tree   The Dish Tree

'The Octopods and Reptiles'

The Octopods and Reptiles
They dine at six o'clock,
And having dined, rush wildly out
  Like an electric shock.
They hang about the bannisters,
The corridors they block,
  And gabbling bothering,
A most unpleasant flock.

They hang about the bannisters,
  Upon the stairs they flock,
And howly-gabbling all the while
  The corridors they block.

[The Heraldic Blazons of Foss the Cat]

Foss Couchant

Foss, a untin.

*Foss
rampant*

Fosh dansant

Fosh, regardant

Foss Pprpr.

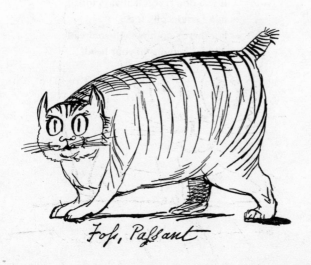

Foss, Passant

'Mrs Jaypher found a wafer'

Mrs Jaypher found a wafer
Which she stuck upon a note;
This she took and gave the cook.
Then she went and bought a boat
Which she paddled down the stream
Shouting, 'Ice produces cream,
Beer when churned produces butter!
Henceforth all the words I utter
Distant ages thus shall note –
From the Jaypher Wisdom-Boat.'

Mrs Jaypher said, 'It's safer,
If you've Lemons in your head,
First to eat a pound of meat,
And then to go at once to bed.
Eating meat is half the battle,
Till you hear the Lemons rattle!
If you don't, you'll always moan;
In a Lemoncolly tone;
For there's nothing half so dread=
=ful, as Lemons in your head!'

From a letter to the Hon. Mrs Augusta Parker

– And my garden is now admirably beautiful, & were it not for the Slugs & Snails would be inimitable. But these melancholy muciliginous Molluscs have eaten up all my Higher-cynths & also my Lower-cynths & I have only just now found a mode of getting rid of these enemies: – which is by flattering their vanity in taking them friendly walks up & down the garden, – an inganno which blinds them to ulterior consequences. And thus, (they being of a monstrous size as you may see by the sketch below,) when I get them near the cistern, I pitch them into the water, where they justly expiate their unpleasant & greedy sins.

[The Later History of the Owl and the Pussy-cat]

My dear Miss Violet,

Your brother Jack goodnaturedly came here yesterday & dined with me, & he brought me a collar from your sister for the Pussy-cat. It was very good of her to think of this, but she evidently has not known, what it is very painful for me to elude to, that the Owl has long been a widower, & that the Pussy I now have is the maternal Uncle of the original Pussy who went to the Bongtree Land.

That party all eventually settled in the North East coast of New Guinea, – the Owl and the Pussy-cat & their 6 children, who are still living & are most lovely & subsequeamish and reprehensible animals, & their subsqueakious history=mystery will some day be exotically & hysterically known to the Public.

The exact details of the death of the original Pussy can now, it seems to me, never be perfectly known. It is certain that she & the Owl staid for more than a month on the Coast of Coromandel with Lady Jingly Jones in a rocky cave, where they led a very happy & hippsipombious life. The next accounts which reached Europe of this estimable creature were that she & her husband the Owl had established themselves in New Guinea, after a vacillating tour to the Seychelles & Madagascar, Mecca, the sauce of the Nile, Amsterdam, Winnipeg, the river Congo & Japan. At New Guinea the whole didactic family were living peaceably, when some savages are said by some of my informants to have suddenly visited their retreat, & to have had long conferences with the Pussy-cat in French, a language which she indiscriminately understood. These visitors went away, but soon afterwards were succeeded by a larger party of persons, who threatened the Pussy-cat most violently with a pair of Tongs & a Pepperbox. In the greatest perplexity she then ran up a tree in company with the Owl, carrying with them a sealed paper, & she was overheard distinctly praying her husband to swallow the document, inasmuch as if found upon them the discovery would insuredly lead to acrostic results. But, – continued my informant, – the Owl positively declined to eat the Paper, whereon the Pussy-cat swallowed it in a rage, and finally – busting into Tears idle Tears, said to her unfortunate husband, – 'My Pœtus! it is not painful!' – (for latterly the Pussy-cat had diligently studied the Roman Bistorians.) Shortly after mutter-uttering these words, she fell off the tree and instantly perspired & became a Copse. It is difficult to imagine the grief of the poor Owl, who immediately disembarked in a sailing vessel & left New Guinea for ever & above: – his grief however was such that it was not possible to get a sufficiently large quantity of Pocket handkerchiefs to wipe his eyes, & they had to cut up the Mainsail & all the other sails for that purpose, – by which untoward fact the vessel could not sail any more, but was wrecked felicitously on the Coast of Cornwall, where the Owl & his children still live though in a bereaved & bohemian condition.

There are however other accounts of the death of the Pussy-cat which are quite different from what I have belated above. For it is said that at New Guinea the brooms with which the family used to sweep out the hole of the tree they inhabited were furnished with handles made of a mellifluous & mucilaginous but highly poisonous sort of wood: & that the Pussy-cat had indulged in a habit of sucking the end of these Broomhandles during intervals of work, & thus imbibed the infectious accusative which ultimately occasioned her dolorific death.

Please to read this letter to your sister Maria, – as slowly & opprobriously as you can in order to save her feelings from a too sudden shock.

    Believe me,
        Yours sincerely,
            Edward Lear.

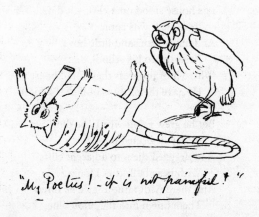

"My Poetus! – it is not painful!"

'When "grand old men" persist in folly'

When 'grand old men' persist in folly
    In slaughtering men and chopping trees,
What art can soothe the melancholy
    Of those whom futile 'statesmen' teaze?

The only way their wrath to cover
    To let mankind know who's to blame ō –
Is first to rush by train to Dover
    And then straight onward to Sanremo.

'He lived at Dingle Bank – he did'

He lived at Dingle Bank – he did; –
    He lived at Dingle Bank;
And in his garden was one Quail,
    Four tulips, and a Tank:
And from his windows he could see
    The otion and the River Dee.

His house stood on a cliff, – it did,
    Its aspic it was cool;
And many thousand little boys
    Resorted to his school,
Where if of progress they could boast
    He gave them heaps of butter'd toast.

But he grew rabid-wroth, he did,
    If they neglected books,
And dragged them to adjacent cliffs
    With beastly Button Hooks,
And there with fatuous glee he threw
    Them down into the otion blue.

And in the sea they swam, they did, –
  All playfully about,   20
And some eventually became
  Sponges, or speckled trout: –
But Liverpool doth all bewail
  Their fate; – likewise his Garden Quail.

'And this is certain; if so be'

And this is certain; if so be
You could just now my garden see,
The aspic of my flowers so bright
Would make you shudder with delight.

And if you voz to see my roziz
As is a boon to all men's noziz, –
You'd fall upon your back and scream –
'O Lawk! o criky! it's a dream!'

Edward Lear
Archbishop of Canterbury
1886

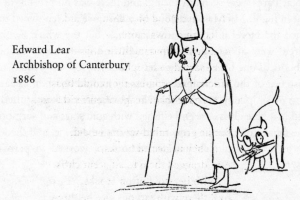

Eggstrax from The Maloja Gazette

It is our painful duty to denounce to a repugnant public, a most fearful clamity which has just occurred to the excellent Mr A. J. Mundella, lately secretary of The Minister of Public destruction. Whatever objections may have been made to some of Mr Mundella's Theories it is impossible to deny that for energy and activity of porpoise, as well as of courtesy and kindliness, he [has] been universally and justly commended. All the more therefore do we egret what has occurred. On quitting his lonerous position, Mr Mundella, with a kindness which those who know him will fully opreciate, proposed to give a substan-
10 tial proof of his interest in the Bore'd Children, by taking them [on] an excursion to Maloja, and having selected 83 of the most surreptitious and balsamic scholars, he accordingly arrived here at the Grand Hotel, accompanied by Mrs and Miss Mundella, and the 83 little boys. The extreme cold of this exalted situation, did not perfectly agree with the systematic stomachs of the children, but Mr and Mrs Mundella took them all out daily on sledges drawn by poodles, – the snow at Maloja being at present over six feet deep. Mr M. was however constantly warned of the danger arising from the pestilent proclivity of the numerous Polar Bears that infect the neighbourhood, a warning – alas!
20 unheeded. For on Friday last, at some distance from the hotel, a drove of Bolar Pares were seen advancing, and there was no prospik of safety but in flight. Mr, Mrs, and Miss Mundella, we are renowned to say, reached the Hotel in contiguous security, – but the whole 83 'bored children' were all snatchell'd up rapidly and destructively devoured. The boots of one little boy alone have been left to Bear witness to the subsistence of the unfortunate scholars: – and these, with a beautiful feeling of simplicity and pathos, Mr Mundella has had stuffed and placed in a blue glass case embellished with gold stars and surmounted by the figures of a sucking pig and a silver stethoscope, and the letters
30 QED as a mucilaginous but merited motto, worked in periwinkle shells.

'When leaving this beautiful blessed Briánza'

When leaving this beautiful blessed Briánza,
   My trunks were all corded and locked except one;
But that was unfilled, through a dismal mancanza,
   Nor could I determine on what should be done.

For out of *three* volumes (all equally bulky),
   Which – travelling, I constantly carry about, –
There was room but for two. So that angry and sulky,
   I had to decide as to which to leave out.

A Bible! A Shakespeare! A Tennyson! – stuffing
   And stamping and squeezing were wholly in vain!   10
A Tennyson! a Shakespeare! a Bible! – all puffing
   Was useless, and one of the three *must* remain.

And this was the end, – (and it's truth and no libel;) –
   A-weary with thinking I settled my doubt,
As I packed and sent off both the Shakespeare and Bible,
   And finally left the 'Lord Tennyson' out.

Some Incidents in the Life of my Uncle Arly

O my agèd Uncle Arly! –
Sitting on a heap of Barley
　　All the silent hours of night, –
Close beside a leafy thicket: –
On his nose there was a Cricket, –
In his hat a Railway Ticket; –
　　(But his shoes were far too tight.)

Long ago, in youth, he squander'd
All his goods away, and wander'd
　　To the Timskoop Hills afar.
There, on golden sunsets blazing
Every evening found him gazing, –
Singing, – 'Orb! you're quite amazing!
　　How I wonder what you are!'

Like the ancient Medes and Persians,
Always by his own exertions
　　He subsisted on those hills; –
Whiles, – by teaching children spelling, –
Or at times by merely yelling, –
Or at intervals by selling
　　'Propter's Nicodemus Pills'.

Later, in his morning rambles
He perceived the moving brambles
　　Something square and white disclose; –
'Twas a First-class Railway-Ticket
But in stooping down to pick it
Off the ground, – a pea-green Cricket
　　Settled on my uncle's Nose.

Never – never more, – oh! never,
Did that Cricket leave him ever, –   30
    Dawn or evening, day or night; –
Clinging as a constant treasure, –
Chirping with a cheerious measure, –
Wholly to my uncle's pleasure, –
    (Though his shoes were far too tight.)

So, for three-and-forty winters,
Till his shoes were worn to splinters,
    All those hills he wander'd o'er, –
Sometimes silent; – sometimes yelling; –
Till he came to Borly-Melling,   40
Near his old ancestral dwelling;–
    – And he wander'd thence no more.

On a little heap of Barley
Died my agèd Uncle Arly,
    And they buried him one night; –
Close beside the leafy thicket; –
There, – his hat and Railway Ticket; –
There, – his ever faithful Cricket; –
    (But his shoes were far too tight.)

'He only said, "I'm very weary'

He only said, 'I'm very weary.'
The rheumatiz he said,
He said, 'It's awful dull and dreary.
I think I'll go to bed.'

I must stop now, as the little gold watch
said when the fat blue-beetle got into his inside.

I think human nature is pretty much the same all along.
On the whole perhaps Pussycat nature is the best.

There was a young lady of Harwich
Who built an astonishing carriage;
It held just a hundred – so every one wondered
And said – What a very odd carriage!! –

There was an old man, whose approach
Was made in a globular coach –
It ran upon reels, instead of on wheels,
And was pulled by a little cockroach.

There was an old lady of Joppa
Who ran so that no one could stop her –
She rushed towards the south
With six pipes in her mouth,
And was never more heard of in Joppa.

There was an old person of Oude –
Who fled when no creature pursued.
When called back by his mother –
He merely said – "bother!" –
That uncivil old person of Oude.

There was an old man of the Rhine,
Who thought it was going to be fine,
So he walked for six hours through wind and through
    showers
That resolute man of the Rhine.

There was an old person of Skye,
Who was nearly a hundred feet high;
He seemed to the people
As tall as a steeple,
And served as a lighthouse in Skye.

There was an old man of Algiers,
Who was given to shedding of tears;
He sate on a rug,
And cried into a jug,
That deplorable man of Algiers. –

There was an old person whose wish
Was to swallow a very large fish –
So he asked his seven daughters
To cut it in quarters,
And boil it for tea in a dish.

Indexes

Index of Titles

Index of First Lines
(Poems, Nonsense Songs and Alphabets)

Subject Index